Modern Critical Interpretations

Modern Critical Interpretations

J. D. Salinger's
The Catcher in the Rye

Edited and with an introduction by
Harold Bloom
Sterling Professor of the Humanities
Yale University

CHELSEA HOUSE PUBLISHERS
Philadelphia

© 2000 by Chelsea House Publishers, a subsidiary of
Haights Cross Communications.

Introduction © 1999 by Harold Bloom

Printed and bound in the United States of America

10 9 8 7 6 5 4 3 2

∞ The paper used in this publication meets the minimum
requirements of the American National Standard for
Permanence of Paper for Printed Library Materials,
Z39.48-1984

Library of Congress Cataloging-in-Publication Data

The catcher in the rye / edited and with an introduction by
Harold Bloom.
     p. cm.— (Modern critical interpretations)
    Includes bibliographical references and index.
    ISBN 0-7910-5664-3
    1. Salinger, J.D. (Jerome David), 1919-Catcher in
the rye.   2. Caulfield, Holden (Fictitious character)
3. Runaway teenagers in literature.   4. Teenage boys in
literature. I. Bloom, Harold. II. Series.
PS3537. A426 C322 2000
813'.54—dc21
                           99-049612
                           CIP

Contributing Editor: Barbara Fischer

Contents

Editor's Note

My Introduction broods on the question of whether *The Catcher in the Rye* someday will be viewed as a period piece.

Holden Caulfield's quest is meditated upon by Arthur Heiserman and James E. Miller Jr.

Salinger's achievement in giving Holden his own parody-language is investigated by Donald P. Costello. Symbolism in the book is described by Clinton W. Trowbridge, while James Bryan engages its psychological structure.

In an adroit essay, Kerry McSweeney revalues *The Catcher in the Rye*, after which Edwin Haviland Miller examines how Holden's grief for his dead brother, Allie, shapes the story.

Holden's relation to Cold War rhetoric is studied by Alan Nadel, while A. Robert Lee considers Holden's status as author.

American protest, rather dormant in 1954, is related to Holden by Joyce Rowe, after which Dennis McCort traces some of *Catcher*'s hidden sources.

In the final essay, Stephen J. Whitfield writes on the ambivalent social reactions that *Catcher* has evoked.

Introduction

It is nearly half-a-century since the publication of *The Catcher in the Rye* (1951), and the short novel has gone through hundreds of printings. Authentic popular fiction of authentic literary distinction is rather rare. Does *The Catcher in the Rye* promise to be of permanent eminence, or will it eventually be seen as an idealistic period-piece, which I think will be the fate of Harper Lee's *To Kill a Mockingbird* and Toni Morrison's *Beloved*, works as popular as *Catcher* continues to be.

The literary ancestors of Holden Caulfield rather clearly include Huck Finn and Gatsby, dangerous influences upon Salinger's novel. *The Adventures of Huckleberry Finn* remains Mark Twain's masterwork, central to Faulkner, Hemingway, Scott Fitzgerald, and the other significant novelists of their generation. *The Great Gatsby* endures as Fitzgerald's classic achievement, capable of many rereadings. Rereading *The Catcher in the Rye* seems to me an aesthetically mixed experience—sometimes poignant, sometimes mawkish or even cloying. Holden's idiom, once established, is self-consistent, but fairly limited in its range and possibilities, perhaps too limited to sustain more than a short story.

And yet Holden retains his pathos, even upon several rereadings. Manhattan has been a descent into Hell for many American writers, most notably in "The Tunnel" section in Hart Crane's visionary epic, *The Bridge*. It becomes Holden's Hell, mostly because of Holden himself, who is masochistic, ambivalent towards women, and acutely ambivalent in regard to his father. Holden's psychic health, already precarious, can barely sustain the stresses of Manhattan. He suffers both from grief at his younger brother Allie's death, and from the irrational guilt of being a survivor.

Holden is seventeen in the novel, but appears not to have matured beyond thirteen, his age when Allie died. Where Holden's distrust of adult language originates, Salinger cannot quite tell us, but the distrust is both noble and self-destructive. To be a catcher in the rye, Holden's ambition, is

1

to be a kind of secular saint, willing and able to save children from disasters.

Faulkner remarked that Holden's dilemma was his inability to find and accept an authentic mentor, a teacher or guide who could arouse his trust. The dilemma, being spiritual, hurts many among us, and is profoundly American. Holden speaks for our skepticism, and for our need. That is a large burden for so fragile a literary character, and will turn out eventually to be either aesthetic salvation for *The Catcher in the Rye*, or a prime cause for its dwindling down to the status of a period piece.

ARTHUR HEISERMAN AND JAMES E. MILLER JR.

J. D. Salinger: Some Crazy Cliff

It is clear that J. D. Salinger's *The Catcher in the Rye* belongs to an ancient and honorable narrative tradition, perhaps the most profound in western fiction. The tradition is the central pattern of the epic and has been enriched by every tongue; for not only is it in itself exciting but also it provides the artist a framework upon which he may hang almost any fabric of events and characters.

It is, of course, the tradition of the Quest. We use the medieval term because it signifies a seeking after what is tremendous, greater than the love of a woman. The love of woman may be part of the seeking, part even of the object sought, for we have been told that the Grail has gender and Penelope did wait in Ithaca. But if the love of woman is essential to the seeking or to the object sought, we must call the search a romance. These two terms (quest and romance) distinguish thematic patterns, and have nothing to do with tragic or comic effects. Furthermore, the same plots, characters, and idioms might be employed inside either pattern. But somewhere upon the arc of the Quest, the love of woman must be eschewed or absorbed: the hero must bind himself to the mast, or must seek his Ducalinda because she is Virtue, not because she is Female.

There are at least two sorts of quests, depending upon the object sought. Stephen Dedalus sought a reality uncontaminated by home, country,

From *Western Humanities Review* 10, no. 2 (Spring 1956). © 1956 University of Utah.

church; for like Eugene Gant and Natty Bumppo he knew that social institutions tend to force what is ingenious in a man into their own channels. He sought the opposite of security, for security was a cataract of the eye. Bloom, on the other hand, was already an outcast and sought acceptance by an Ithaca and a Penelope which despised him. And, tragically enough, he also sought an Icarian son who had fled the very same maze which he, Bloom, desired to enter. So the two kinds of quests, the one seeking acceptance and stability, the other precisely the opposite, differ significantly, and can cross only briefly to the drunken wonder of both heroes. Bloom, the protagonist of *The Waste Land*, the Joads, Alyosha Karamazov, Aeneas, Ulysses, Gatsby—these heroes seek acceptance, stability, a life enbosomed upon what is known and can be trusted. Dedalus, Huck Finn, Ishmael, Hans Castorp, Huxley's heroes, Dostoevski's Idiot—these protagonists place themselves outside the bounds of what is known and seek not stability but a Truth which is unwarped by stability.

American literature seems fascinated with the outcast, the person who defies traditions in order to arrive at some pristine knowledge, some personal integrity. Natty Bumppo maintains his integrity out-of-doors only, for upon the frontier a man must be a man or perish. For Huck Finn both sides of the Mississippi are lined with fraud and hatred; and because the great brown river acts as a kind of sewer, you're liable to find murderers and thieves afloat on it—even the father whom you fled might turn up dead in it, as though the river were a dream. But in the middle of the great natural river, when you're naked of civilization and in company with an outcast more untarnished and childlike than yourself—*there* is peace. And in northern Mississippi, in the ante-Snopes era, frontiersmen conquer the wilderness using only their courage and their fury; and they behave, even when civilization has almost extinguished them, with the kind of insane honor that drives Quentin Compson outside of society and into suicide. And the hunter, as he tracks the great mythic bear or the incredible whale, must leave behind whatever is unnatural or convenient. Similarly, when the bull charges, you are faced with the same compulsion for integrity as is required by the wilderness, the whale, the bear, the river; and very often, the world so botches things that you must "make a separate peace" in order to maintain your moral entity intact.

All the virtues of these American heroes are personal ones: they most often, as a matter of fact, are in conflict with home, family, church. The typical American hero must flee these institutions, become a tramp in the earth, cut himself off from Chicago, Winesburg, Hannibal, Cooperstown, New York, Asheville, Minneapolis. For only by flight can he find knowledge of what is real. And if he does not flee, he at least defies.

The protagonist of *The Catcher in the Rye*, Holden Caulfield, is one of these American heroes, but with a significant difference. He seems to be engaged in both sorts of quests at once; he needs to go home and he needs to leave it. Unlike the other American knight errants, Holden seeks Virtue second to Love. He wants to be good. When the little children are playing in the rye-field on the clifftop, Holden wants to be the one who catches them before they fall off the cliff. He is not driven toward honor or courage. He is not driven toward love of woman. Holden is driven toward love of his fellow-man, charity—virtues which were perhaps not quite virile enough for Natty Bumppo, Ishmael, Huck Finn, or Nick Adams. Holden is actually frightened by a frontier code of masculinity—a code which sometimes requires its adherents to behave in sentimental and bumptious fashions. But like these American heroes, Holden is a wanderer, for in order to be good he has to be more of a bad boy than the puritanical Huck could have imagined. Holden has had enough of both Hannibal, Missouri, *and* the Mississippi; and his tragedy is that when he starts back up the river, he has no place to go—save, of course, a California psychiatrist's couch.

So Salinger translates the old tradition into contemporary terms. The phoniness of society forces Holden Caulfield to leave it, but he is seeking nothing less than stability and love. He would like nothing better than a home, a life embosomed upon what is known and can be trusted; he is a very wise sheep forced into lone wolf's clothing; he is Stephen Dedalus and Leopold Bloom rolled into one crazy kid. And here is the point; for poor Holden, there is no Ithaca. Ithaca has not merely been defiled by a horde of suitors: it has sunk beneath waves of phoniness. He does, of course, have a Penelope who is still intact. She is his little sister Phoebe whom he must protect at all costs from the phantoms of lust, hypocrisy, conceit and fear— all of the attributes which Holden sees in society and which Huck Finn saw on the banks of the Mississippi and Dedalus saw in Dublin. So at the end, like the hero of *Antic Hay*, Holden delights in circles—a comforting, bounded figure which yet connotes hopelessness. He breaks down as he watches his beloved little Phoebe going round and round on a carousel; she is so *damned* happy. From that lunatic delight in a circle, he is shipped off to the psychiatrist. For Holden loves the world more than the world can bear.

Holden's Quest takes him outside society; yet the grail he seeks is the world and the grail is full of love. To be a catcher in the rye in this world is possible only at the price of leaving it. To be good is to be a "case," a "bad boy" who confounds the society of men. So Holden seeks the one role which would allow him to be a catcher, and that role is the role of the child. As a child, he would be condoned, for a child is a sort of savage and a pariah because he is innocent and good. But it is Holden's tragedy that he is sixteen, and like Wordsworth he can never be less. In childhood he had what he is now seeking—non-phoniness, truth, innocence. He can find it now only in Phoebe and in his dead brother Allie's baseball mitt, in a red hunting cap and the tender little nuns. Still, unlike all of us, Holden refuses to compromise with adulthood and its necessary adulteries; and his heroism drives him berserk. Huck Finn had the Mississippi and at the end of the Mississippi he had the wild west beyond Arkansas. The hero of *The Waste Land* had Shantih, the peace which passes human understanding. Bloom had Molly and his own ignorance; Dedalus had Paris and Zurich. But for Holden, there is no place to go.

II

The central theme of Salinger's work is stated explicitly in one of his best short stories, "For Esme—with Love and Squalor." Salinger quotes a passage from Dostoevski: "Fathers and teachers, I ponder 'What is Hell?' I maintain that it is the suffering of being unable to love."

The hero of "For Esme" is an American soldier who, driven too near psychosis by five campaigns of World War II and a moronic jeepmate, is saved in an act of childish love by two remarkable English children. Just as surely as war and neurosis are both manifestations of the lack of love, the soldier discovers peace and happiness are manifestations of love's presence. This Love must be spelled with a capital; for it is not the alienated, romantic love of the courtly romances and "Dover Beach"—a love which is tragic because it is founded upon Eros; but rather it is the expansive, yea-saying love of all Creation which we find in the saints and which is never tragic because it is founded upon Agape. This love is the dominant trait of all Salinger's heroes, and when it is thwarted the hero either shoots himself, as does the veteran with "battle fatigue" in "A Perfect Day for Bananafish," or goes berserk or melancholic as do the heroes of *The Catcher in the Rye* and "Uncle Wiggily in Connecticut." But when, on the other hand, a person finds a way to love the world, then that person is saved from madness and suicide as is the soldier in "For Esme." Salinger thus diagnoses the neurosis and fatigue of the world in one simple way: if we cannot love, we cannot live.

Childhood and the loss of innocence have obsessed much of western literature at least since the Enlightenment, when man was declared innately good, corrupted only by his institutions. If we could return to childhood, or to noble savagery; or if we could retain the spontaneity of childhood, our social and personal problems would disappear. Emile, Candide, the young Wordsworth, Huck Finn, Holden Caulfield—all lament or seek a return to a lost childhood for precisely the same reasons that one is forced to make peace with one's childhood on the analyst's couch, or that the Marxist must look with a sigh upon Eden, where the fruits of production were consumed entirely by their tenders. Each of us does indeed carry an Adam inside us, whether he be Original Sin or Innocence: and the modern world has for the most part judged him innocent. Yet the clouds of glory which we trailed dwindle and turn back in adulthood; for when the world was new, before the pimples appeared, it was with us not too much but utterly and we could love it innocently, without fear. Of course, what Wordsworth remembered above Tintern Abbey, what Clemens recalled in New York, what Rousseau attempted to breed in France, what modern art attempted to recreate from Negro and Oriental models, never really existed in pure form in the first place. How horrified Wordsworth would have been had he learned what romanticism's dank blossom, Freud, discovered in the dictum that "the child is father of the man"! Nevertheless, as Freud made Childism clinical he also made it rampant; and the initiation story, the fable of Innocence Lost, has developed into a dominant motif in contemporary fiction.

The flight out of the world, out of the ordinary, and into an Eden of innocence or childhood is a common flight indeed, and it is one which Salinger's heroes are constantly attempting. But Salinger's childism is consubstantial with his concern for love and neurosis. Adultism is precisely "the suffering of being unable to love," and it is that which produces neurosis. Everyone able to love in Salinger's stories is either a child or a man influenced by a child. All the adults not informed by love and innocence are by definition phonies and prostitutes. "You take adults, they always look lousy when they're asleep with their mouths open, but kids don't . . . They look all right." Kids like Phoebe shut up when they haven't anything to say. They even say "thank you" when you tighten their skates, and they don't go behind a post to button their pants. The nuns expect no swanky lunches after standing on a corner to collect money. Young James Castle would not go back on his word even though he had to jump from a window to keep it.

Holden is the kind of person who feels sorry for the teachers who have to flunk him. He fears for the ducks when the lagoon freezes over, for he is a duck himself with no place to go. He must enter his own home like a crook, lying to elevator boys and tip-toeing past bedrooms. His dad "will kill" him and his mother will weep for his incorrigible "laziness." He wants only to pretend he is a deaf-mute and live as a hermit filling-station operator in Colorado, but he winds up where the frontier ends, California, in an institution for sick rich kids. And we can see, on the final note of irony in the book, that that frontier west which represented escape from "sivilization" for Huck Finn has ended by becoming the symbol for depravity and phoniness in our national shrine at Hollywood.

III

The most distinctive aspect of Salinger's humor is its invariable effect of intensifying poignance and even horror. At the end of "A Perfect Day for Bananafish," Seymour Glass, the sensitive young protagonist, is unable to reconcile himself to the evil adult world into which he has been thrust, with its brutal wars and sordid and even hateful relationships with a shallow-headed wife and her self-centered family. Even the steadying influence of the genuine innocence of little Sybil Carpenter is not sufficient to deter Seymour from his will to self-destruction. As he is on his way to his room at the end of the story, he boards the hotel elevator and believes that one of his fellow passengers is scrutinizing him. "I see you're looking at my feet," he says, and the startled woman with zinc salve on her nose replies, "I *beg* your pardon?" But the young man has become acutely sensitive: "If you want to look at my feet, say so. . . . But don't be a God-damned sneak about it."

The story at this point is simultaneously at its funniest and its most poignant. In less than one brief page the young man is dead: "Then he went over and sat down on the unoccupied twin bed, looked at the girl, aimed the pistol, and fired a bullet through his right temple." The close juxtaposition of these two passages, the one a height in comic incongruity, the other a depth in tragic action, works a unique effect. The comic element intensifies rather than relieves the tragic. As we observe the young man raise the pistol to his head, we are horrified that we have just been laughing at his extreme sensitivity about his feet. Perhaps we even have the guilty feeling of having ridiculed a deformity—a deformity of the spirit. In any event we are stunned into a keen realization of the tragic human plight.

It is this poignance which characterizes all of Salinger's humor, this catch in the throat that accompanies all of the laughs. Holden Caulfield is no clown nor is he a tragic hero; he is a sixteen-year-old lad whose vivid encounter with everyday life is tragically humorous—or humorously tragic. At the end of the novel, as we leave Holden in the psychiatric ward of the California hospital, we come to the realization that the abundant and richly varied humor of the novel has reenforced the serious intensity of Holden's frantic flight from Adultism and his frenzied search for the genuine in a terrifyingly phony world.

Holden Caulfield, like Huckleberry Finn, tells his own story and it is in the language of the telling in both books that a great part of the humor lies. In the nineteenth century, Huck began, "You don't know about me without you have read a book by the name of *The Adventures of Tom Sawyer:* but that ain't no matter." The English of Huck's twentieth century counterpart, Holden Caulfield, is perhaps more correct but nonetheless distinctive: "If you really want to hear about it, the first thing you'll probably want to know is where I was born, and what my lousy childhood was like, and how my parents were occupied and all before they had me, and all that David Copperfield kind of crap, but I don't feel like going into it, if you want to know the truth."

The skepticism inherent in that casual phrase, "if you want to know the truth," suggesting that as a matter of fact in the world of Holden Caulfield very few people do, characterizes this sixteen-year-old "crazy mixed up kid" more sharply and vividly than pages of character "analysis" possibly could. In a similar manner Huck's "that ain't no matter" speaks volumes for his relationship in the alien adult world in which he finds himself a sojourner. But if these two boys lay their souls bare by their own voices, in doing so they provoke smiles at their mishandling and sometimes downright mangling of the English language.

Huck's spelling of *sivilization* gives the word a look which makes what it stands for understandably distasteful. Holden's incorrectness frequently appears to be a straining after correctness ("She'd give Allie or I a push. . . .") which suggests a subconcious will to non-conformity. But the similarities of language of Huck and Holden are balanced by marked differences. Both boys are fugitives from education, but Holden has suffered more of the evil than Huck. Holden's best subject in the several schools he has tolerated briefly is English. And, too, Holden is a child of the twentieth century. Mark Twain himself would probably be startled not at the frankness of Holden's language but at the daring of J. D. Salinger in copying it so faithfully.

But of course neither J. D. Salinger nor Mark Twain really "copied" anything. Their books would be unreadable had they merely recorded intact the language of a real-life Huck and a real-life Holden. Their genius lies in their mastery of the technique of first person narration which, through meticulous selection, creates vividly the illusion of life: gradually and subtly their narrators emerge and stand revealed, stripped to their innermost beings. It is a mark of their creators' mastery that Huck and Holden appear to reveal themselves.

It is not the least surprising aspect of *The Catcher in the Rye* that trite expressions and metaphors with which we are all familiar and even bored turn out, when emerging from the mouth of a sixteen-year-old, to be funny. The unimaginative repetition of identical expressions in countless situations intensifies the humor. The things in Holden's world are always jumping up and down or bouncing or scattering "like madmen." Holden always lets us know when he has insight into the absurdity of the endless absurd situations which make up the life of a sixteen-year-old by exclaiming, "It killed me." In a phony world Holden feels compelled to reenforce his sincerity and truthfulness constantly with "It really is" or "It really did." Incongruously the adjective "old" serves as a term of endearment, from "old" Thomas Hardy to "old" Phoebe. And many of the things Holden does, he does, ambiguously, "like a bastard."

Holden is a master of the ludicrous irrelevancy. Indeed, a large part of *The Catcher in the Rye* consists of the relevantly irrelevant. On the opening page, Holden says, "I'm not going to tell you my whole goddam autobiography or anything. I'll just tell you about this madman stuff that happened to me around last Christmas. . . ." By the time we have finished *Catcher* we feel that we know Holden as thoroughly as any biography could reveal him, and one of the reasons is that he has not hesitated to follow in his tale wherever whim and fancy lead him. For example, in the early part of the novel, Holden goes at some length into the history of the Ossenburger Memorial Wing of the new dorms, his place of residence. Ossenburger, we are told, was the Pencey alumnus who made a "pot of dough" in the undertaking business, and who, after giving money to Pencey, gave a speech in chapel "that lasted about ten hours." "He told us we should always pray to God—talk to him and all—wherever we were. He told us we ought to think of Jesus as our buddy and all. He said *he* talked to Jesus all of the time. Even when he was driving his car. That killed me. I can just see the big phony bastard shifting into first gear and asking Jesus to send him a few more stiffs." Ossenburger, of course, has nothing to do, directly, with the "madman stuff" that happened to Holden around Christmas; but Holden's value judgment of the phony Ossenburger is certainly relevant to Salinger's purpose, the revelation of Holden's character.

When Holden refuses to express aggressive dislike of the repulsive Ackley, the pimply boy whose teeth "looked mossy and awful," he is not being facetious nor is he lying. He is simply expressing an innocence incapable of genuine hatred. Holden does not suffer from the inability to love, but he does despair of finding a place to bestow his love. The depth of Holden's capacity for love is revealed in his final words, as he sits in the psychiatric ward musing over his nightmarish adventures: "If you want to know the truth, I don't *know* what I think about it. I'm sorry I told so many people about it. About all I know is, I sort of miss everybody I told about. Even old Stradlater and Ackley, for instance. I think I even miss that goddam Maurice. It's funny. Don't ever tell anybody anything. If you do, you start missing everybody." We agree with Holden that it is funny, but it is funny in a pathetic kind of way. As we leave Holden alone in his room in the psychiatric ward, we are aware of the book's last ironic incongruity. It is not Holden who should be examined for a sickness of the mind, but the world in which he has sojourned and found himself an alien. To "cure" Holden, he must be given the contagious, almost universal disease of phony adultism; he must be pushed over that "crazy cliff."

DONALD P. COSTELLO

The Language of The Catcher in the Rye

A study of the language of J. D. Salinger's *The Catcher in the Rye* can be justified not only on the basis of literary interest, but also on the basis of linguistic significance. Today we study *The Adventures of Huckleberry Finn* (with which many critics have compared *The Catcher in the Rye*) not only as a great work of literary art, but as a valuable study in 1884 dialect. In coming decades, *The Catcher in the Rye* will be studied, I feel, not only as a literary work, but also as an example of teenage vernacular in the 1950s. As such, the book will be a significant historical linguistic record of a type of speech rarely made available in permanent form. Its linguistic importance will increase as the American speech it records becomes less current.

Most critics who looked at *The Catcher in the Rye* at the time of its publication thought that its language was a true and authentic rendering of teenage colloquial speech. Reviewers in the Chicago *Sunday Tribune*, the London *Times Literary Supplement*, the *New Republic*, the New York *Herald Tribune Book Review*, the New York *Times*, the *New Yorker*, and the *Saturday Review of Literature* all specifically mentioned the authenticity of the book's language. Various aspects of its language were also discussed in the reviews published in *America*, the *Atlantic*, the *Catholic World*, the *Christian Science Monitor*, the *Library Journal*, the Manchester *Guardian*, the *Nation*, the *New Statesman and Nation*, the New York *Times Book Review*, *Newsweek*, the

From *American Speech* 34, no. 3 (October 1959). © 1959 Columbia University Press.

Spectator, and *Time.* Of these many reviews, only the writers for the *Catholic World* and the *Christian Science Monitor* denied the authenticity of the book's language, but both of these are religious journals which refused to believe that the 'obscenity' was realistic. An examination of the reviews of *The Catcher in the Rye* proves that the language of Holden Caulfield, the book's sixteen-year-old narrator, struck the ear of the contemporary reader as an accurate rendering of the informal speech of an intelligent, educated, Northeastern American adolescent.

In addition to commenting on its authenticity, critics have often remarked—uneasily—the 'daring,' 'obscene,' 'blasphemous' features of Holden's language. Another commonly noted feature of the book's language has been its comic effect. And yet there has never been an extensive investigation of the language itself. That is what this paper proposes to do.

Even though Holden's language is authentic teenage speech, recording it was certainly not the major intention of Salinger. He was faced with the artistic task of creating an individual character, not with the linguistic task of reproducing the exact speech of teenagers in general. Yet Holden had to speak a recognizable teenage language, and at the same time had to be identifiable as an individual. This difficult task Salinger achieved by giving Holden an extremely trite and typical teenage speech, overlaid with strong personal idiosyncracies. There are two major speech habits which are Holden's own, which are endlessly repeated throughout the book, and which are, nevertheless, typical enough of teenage speech so that Holden can be both typical and individual in his use of them. It is certainly common for teenagers to end thoughts with a loosely dangling 'and all,' just as it is common for them to add an insistent 'I really did,' 'It really was.' But Holden uses these phrases to such an overpowering degree that they become a clear part of the flavor of the book; they become, more, a part of Holden himself, and actually help to characterize him.

Holden's 'and all' and its twins 'or something,' 'or anything,' serve no real, consistent linguistic function. They simply give a sense of looseness of expression and looseness of thought. Often they signify that Holden knows there is more that could be said about the issue at hand, but he is not going to bother going into it.

> . . . how my parents were occupied and all before they had me

> . . . they're *nice* and all

> I'm not going to tell you my whole goddam autobiography or anything

. . . splendid and clear-thinking and all

But just as often the use of such expressions is purely arbitrary, with no discernible meaning:

. . . he's my *brother* and all

. . . was in the Revolutionary War and all

It was December and all

. . . no gloves or anything

. . . right in the pocket and all

Donald Barr, writing in the *Commonweal*, finds this habit indicative of Holden's tendency to generalize, to find the all in the one:

> Salinger has an ear not only for idiosyncrasies of diction and syntax, but for mental processes. Holden Caulfield's phrase is 'and all'—'She looked so damn *nice*, the way she kept going around and around in her blue coat and all'—as if each experience wore a halo. His fallacy is *ab uno disce omnes*; he abstracts and generalizes wildly.

Heiserman and Miller, in the *Western Humanities Review*, comment specifically upon Holden's second most obvious idiosyncrasy: 'In a phony world Holden feels compelled to reenforce his sincerity and truthfulness constantly with "It really is" or "It really did."' S. N. Behrman, in the *New Yorker*, finds a double function of these 'perpetual insistences of Holden's.' Berhman thinks they 'reveal his age, even when he is thinking much older,' and, more important, 'he is so aware of the danger of slipping into phoniness himself that he has to repeat over and over "I really mean it," "It really does."' Holden uses this idiosyncrasy of insistence almost every time that he makes an affirmation.

Allied to Holden's habit of insistence is his 'if you want to know the truth.' Heiserman and Miller are able to find characterization in this habit too:

> The skepticism inherent in that casual phrase, 'if you want to know the truth,' suggesting that as a matter of fact in the world of Holden Caulfield very few people do, characterizes this

sixteen-year-old 'crazy mixed up kid' more sharply and vividly
than pages of character 'analysis' possibly could.

Holden uses this phrase only after affirmations, just as he uses 'It really does,'
but usually after the personal ones, where he is consciously being frank:

> I have no wind, if you want to know the truth.
>   I don't even think that bastard had a handkerchief, if
> you want to know the truth.
>   I'm a pacifist, if you want to know the truth.
>   She had quite a lot of sex appeal, too, if you really
> want to know.
>   I was damn near bawling, I felt so damn happy, if
> you want to know the truth.

These personal idiosyncrasies of Holden's speech are in keeping with
general teenage language. Yet they are so much a part of Holden and of the
flavor of the book that they are much of what makes Holden to be Holden.
They are the most memorable feature of the book's language. Although
always in character, the rest of Holden's speech is more typical than
individual. The special quality of this language comes from its triteness, its
lack of distinctive qualities.

Holden's informal, schoolboy vernacular is particularly typical in its
'vulgarity' and 'obscenity.' No one familiar with prep-school speech could
seriously contend that Salinger overplayed his hand in this respect. On the
contrary, Holden's restraints help to characterize him as a sensitive youth who
avoids the most strongly forbidden terms, and who never uses vulgarity in a self-
conscious or phony way to help him be 'one of the boys.' *Fuck*, for example, is
never used as a part of Holden's speech. The word appears in the novel four
times, but only when Holden disapprovingly discusses its wide appearance on
walls. The Divine name is used habitually by Holden only in the comparatively
weak *for God's sake, God,* and *goddam.* The stronger and usually more offensive
for Chrissake or *Jesus* or *Jesus Christ* are used habitually by Ackley and Stradlater;
but Holden uses them only when he feels the need for a strong expression. He
almost never uses *for Chrissake* in an unemotional situation. *Goddam* is Holden's
favorite adjective. This word is used with no relationship to its original
meaning, or to Holden's attitude toward the word to which it is attached. It
simply expresses an emotional feeling toward the object: either favorable, as in
'goddam hunting cap'; or unfavorable, as in 'ya goddam moron'; or indifferent,
as in 'coming in the goddam windows.' *Damn* is used interchangably with
goddam; no differentation in its meaning is detectable.

Other crude words are also often used in Holden's vocabulary. *Ass* keeps a fairly restricted meaning as a part of the human anatomy, but it is used in a variety of ways. It can refer simply to that specific part of the body ('I moved my ass a little'), or be part of a trite expression ('freezing my ass off'; 'in a half-assed way'), or be expletive ('Game, my ass.'). *Hell* is perhaps the most versatile word in Holden's entire vocabulary; it serves most of the meanings and constructions which Mencken lists in his *American Speech* article on 'American Profanity.' So far is Holden's use of *hell* from its original meaning that he can use the sentence 'We had a helluva time' to mean that he and Phoebe had a decidedly pleasant time downtown shopping for shoes. The most common function of *hell* is as the second part of a simile, in which a thing can be either 'hot as hell' or, strangely, 'cold as hell'; 'sad as hell' or 'playful as hell'; 'old as hell' or 'pretty as hell.' Like all of these words, *hell* has no close relationship to its original meaning.

Both *bastard* and *sonuvabitch* have also drastically changed in meaning. They no longer, of course, in Holden's vocabulary, have any connection with the accidents of birth. Unless used in a trite simile, *bastard* is a strong word, reserved for things and people Holden particularly dislikes, especially 'phonies.' *Sonuvabitch* has an even stronger meaning to Holden; he uses it only in the deepest anger. When, for example, Holden is furious with Stradlater over his treatment of Jane Gallagher, Holden repeats again and again that he 'kept calling him a moron sonuvabitch.'

The use of crude language in *The Catcher in the Rye* increases, as we should expect, when Holden is reporting schoolboy dialogue. When he is directly addressing the reader, Holden's use of such language drops off almost entirely. There is also an increase in this language when any of the characters are excited or angry. Thus, when Holden is apprehensive over Stradlater's treatment of Jane, his *goddams* increase suddenly to seven on a single page.

Holden's speech is also typical in his use of slang. I have catalogued over a hundred slang terms used by Holden, and every one of these is in widespread use. Although Holden's slang is rich and colorful, it, of course, being slang, often fails at precise communication. Thus, Holden's *crap* is used in seven different ways. It can mean foolishness, as 'all that David Copperfield kind of crap,' or messy matter, as 'I spilled some crap all over my gray flannel,' or merely miscellaneous matter, as 'I was putting on my galoshes and crap.' It can also carry its basic meaning, animal excreta, as 'there didn't look like there was anything in the park except dog crap,' and it can be used as an adjective meaning anything generally unfavorable, as 'The show was on the crappy side.' Holden uses the phrases *to be a lot of crap* and *to shoot the crap* and *to chuck the crap* all to mean 'to be untrue,' but he can also use *to shoot the crap* to mean simply 'to chat,' with no connotation of untruth, as in 'I certainly wouldn't have minded shooting the crap with old Phoebe for a while.'

Similarly Holden's slang use of *crazy* is both trite and imprecise. 'That drives me crazy' means that he violently dislikes something; yet 'to be crazy about' something means just the opposite. In the same way, to be 'killed' by something can mean that he was emotionally affected either favorably ('That story just about killed me.') or unfavorably ('Then she turned her back on me again. It nearly killed me.'). This use of *killed* is one of Holden's favorite slang expressions. Heiserman and Miller are, incidentally, certainly incorrect when they conclude: 'Holden always lets us know when he has insight into the absurdity of the endlessly absurd situations which make up the life of a sixteen-year-old by exclaiming, "It killed me."' Holden often uses this expression with no connection to the absurd; he even uses it for his beloved Phoebe. The expression simply indicates a high degree of emotion—any kind. It is hazardous to conclude that any of Holden's slang has a precise and consistent meaning or function. These same critics fall into the same error when they conclude that Holden's use of the adjective *old* serves as 'a term of endearment.' Holden appends this word to almost every character, real or fictional, mentioned in the novel, from the hated 'old Maurice' to 'old Peter Lorre,' to 'old Phoebe,' and even 'old Jesus.' The only pattern that can be discovered in Holden's use of this term is that he usually uses it only after he has previously mentioned the character; he then feels free to append the familiar *old*. All we can conclude from Holden's slang is that it is typical teenage slang: versatile yet narrow, expressive yet unimaginative, imprecise, often crude, and always trite.

Holden has many favorite slang expressions which he overuses. In one place, he admits:

> 'Boy!' I said. I also say 'Boy!' quite a lot. Partly because I have
> a lousy vocabulary and partly because I act quite young for my
> age sometimes.

But if Holden's slang shows the typically 'lousy vocabulary' of even the educated American teenager, this failing becomes even more obvious when we narrow our view to Holden's choice of adjectives and adverbs. The choice is indeed narrow, with a constant repetition of a few favorite words: *lousy, pretty, crumby, terrific, quite, old, stupid*—all used, as is the habit of teenage vernacular, with little regard to specific meaning. Thus, most of the nouns which are called 'stupid' could not in any logical framework be called 'ignorant,' and, as we have seen, *old* before a proper noun has nothing to do with age.

Another respect in which Holden was correct in accusing himself of having a 'lousy vocabulary' is discovered in the ease with which he falls into trite figures of speech. We have already seen that Holden's most common simile is the worn and meaningless 'as hell'; but his often-repeated 'like a madman' and 'like a bastard' are just about as unrelated to a literal meaning and are easily as unimaginative. Even Holden's nonhabitual figures of speech are usually trite: 'sharp as a tack'; 'hot as a firecracker'; 'laughed like a hyena'; 'I know old Jane like a book'; 'drove off like a bat out of hell'; 'I began to feel like a horse's ass'; 'blind as a bat'; 'I know Central Park like the back of my hand.'

Repetitious and trite as Holden's vocabulary may be, it can, nevertheless, become highly effective. For example, when Holden piles one trite adjective upon another, a strong power of invective is often the result:

> He was a goddam stupid moron.
> Get your dirty stinking moron knees of my chest.
> You're a dirty stupid sonuvabitch of a moron.

And his limited vocabulary can also be used for good comic effect. Holden's constant repetition of identical expressions in countless widely different situations is often hilariously funny.

But all of the humor in Holden's vocabulary does not come from its unimaginative quality. Quite the contrary, some of his figures of speech are entirely original; and these are inspired, dramatically effective, and terribly funny. As always, Salinger's Holden is basically typical, with a strong overlay of the individual:

> He started handling my exam paper like it was a turd or something.
> He put my goddam paper down then and looked at me like he'd just beaten the hell out of me in ping-pong or something.
> That guy Morrow was about as sensitive as a toilet seat.
> Old Marty was like dragging the Statue of Liberty around the floor.

Another aspect in which Holden's language is typical is that it shows the general American characteristic of adaptability—apparently strengthened by his teenage lack of restraint. It is very easy for Holden to turn nouns into adjectives, with the simple addition of a -*y*: 'perverty,' 'Christmasy,' 'vomity-looking,' 'whory-looking,' 'hoodlumy-looking,' 'show-offy,' 'flitty-looking,' 'dumpy-looking,' 'pimpy,' 'snobby,' 'fisty.' Like all of English, Holden's language shows a versatile combining ability: 'They gave Sally this little blue butt-twitcher of a dress to wear' and 'That magazine was some little cheerer upper.' Perhaps the most interesting aspect of the adaptability of Holden's language is his ability to use nouns as adverbs: 'She sings it very Dixieland and whorehouse, and it doesn't sound at all mushy.'

As we have seen, Holden shares, in general, the trite repetitive vocabulary which is the typical lot of his age group. But as there are exceptions in his figures of speech, so are there exceptions in his vocabulary itself, in his word stock. An intelligent, well-read ('I'm quite illiterate, but I read a lot'), and educated boy, Holden possesses, and can use when he wants to, many words which are many a cut above Basic English, including 'ostracized,' 'exhibitionist,' 'unscrupulous,' 'conversationalist,' 'psychic,' 'bourgeois.' Often Holden seems to choose his words consciously, in an effort to communicate to the reader clearly and properly, as in such terms as 'lose my virginity,' 'relieve himself,' 'an alcoholic'; for upon occasion, he also uses the more vulgar terms 'to give someone the time,' 'to take a leak,' 'booze hound.' Much of the humor arises, in fact, from Holden's habit of writing on more than one level at the same time. Thus, we have such phrases as 'They give guys the ax quite frequently at Pencey' and 'It has a very good academic rating, Pencey.' Both sentences show a colloquial idiom with an overlay of consciously selected words.

Such a conscious choice of words seems to indicate that Salinger, in his attempt to create a realistic character in Holden, wanted to make him aware of his speech, as, indeed, a real teenager would be when communicating to the outside world. Another piece of evidence is that Holden is conscious of his speech and, more, realizes a difficulty in communication, is found in his habit of direct repetition: 'She likes me a lot. I mean she's quite fond of me,' and 'She can be very snotty sometimes. She can be quite snotty.' Sometimes the repetition is exact: 'He was a very nervous guy—I mean he was a very nervous guy,' and 'I sort of missed them. I mean I sort of missed them.' Sometimes Holden stops specifically to interpret slang terms, as when he wants to communicate that Allie liked Phoebe: 'She killed Allie, too. I mean he liked her, too.'

There is still more direct evidence that Holden was conscious of his speech. Many of his comments to the reader are concerned with language. He was aware, for example, of the 'phony' quality of many words and phrases, such as 'grand,' 'prince,' 'traveling incognito,' 'little girl's room,' 'licorice stick,' and 'angels.' Holden is also conscious, of course, of the existence of 'taboo words.' He makes a point of mentioning that the girl from Seattle repeatedly asked him to 'watch your language, if you don't mind,' and that his mother told Phoebe not to say 'lousy.' When the prostitute says 'Like fun you are,' Holden comments:

> It was a funny thing to say. It sounded like a real kid. You'd think a prostitute and all would say 'Like hell you are' or 'Cut the crap' instead of 'Like fun you are.'

In grammar, too, as in vocabulary, Holden possesses a certain self-consciousness. (It is, of course, impossible to imagine a student getting through today's schools without a self-consciousness with regard to grammar rules.) Holden is, in fact, not only aware of the existence of 'grammatical errors,' but knows the social taboos that accompany them. He is disturbed by a schoolmate who is ashamed of his parents' grammar, and he reports that his former teacher, Mr. Antolini, warned him about picking up 'just enough education to hate people who say, "It's a secret between he and I."'

Holden is a typical enough teenager to violate the grammar rules, even though he knows of their social importance. His most common rule violation is the misuse of *lie* and *lay*, but he also is careless about relative pronouns ('about a traffic cop that falls in love'), the double negative ('I hardly didn't even know I was doing it'), the perfect tenses ('I'd woke him up'), extra words ('like as if all you ever did at Pencey was play polo all the time'), pronoun number ('it's pretty disgusting to watch somebody picking their nose'), and pronoun position ('I and this friend of mine, Mal Brossard'). More remarkable, however, than the instances of grammar rule violations is Holden's relative 'correctness.' Holden is always intelligible, and is even 'correct' in many usually difficult constructions. Gramatically speaking, Holden's language seems to point up the fact that English was the only subject in which he was not failing. It is interesting to note how much more 'correct' Holden's speech is than that of Huck Finn. But then Holden is educated, and since the time of Huck there had been sixty-seven years of authoritarian schoolmarms working on the likes of Holden. He has, in fact, been overtaught, so that he uses many 'hyper' forms:

> I used to play tennis with he and Mrs. Antolini quite frequently.
> She'd give Allie or I a push.
> I and Allie used to take her to the park with us.
> I think I probably woke he and his wife up.

Now that we have examined several aspects of Holden's vocabulary and grammar, it would be well to look at a few examples of how he puts these elements together into sentences. The structure of Holden's sentences indicates that Salinger thinks of the book more in terms of spoken speech than written speech. Holden's faulty structure is quite common and typical in vocal expression; I doubt if a student who is 'good in English' would ever create such sentence structure in writing. A student who showed the self-consciousness of Holden would not *write* so many fragments, such afterthoughts (e.g., 'It has a very good academic rating, Pencey'), or such repetitions (e.g., 'Where I lived at Pencey, I lived in the Ossenburger Memorial Wing of the new dorms').

There are other indications that Holden's speech is vocal. In many places, Salinger mildly imitates spoken speech. Sentences such as 'You could tell old Spencer'd got a big bang out of buying it' and 'I'd've killed him' are repeated throughout the book. Yet it is impossible to imagine Holden taking pen in hand and actually writing 'Spencer'd' or 'I'd've.' Sometimes, too, emphasized words, or even parts of words, are italicized, as in 'Now *shut up*, Holden. God damn it—I'm *warn*ing ya.' This is often done with good effect, imitating quite perfectly the rhythms of speech, as in the typical:

> I practically sat down on her *lap*, as a matter of fact. Then she *really* started to cry, and the next thing I knew, I was kissing her all over—*any*where—her eyes, her *nose*, her forehead, her eyebrows and all, her *ears*—her whole face except for her mouth and all.

The language of *The Catcher in the Rye* is, as we have seen, an authentic artistic rendering of a type of informal, colloquial, teenage American spoken speech. It is strongly typical and trite, yet often somewhat individual; it is crude and slangy and imprecise, imitative yet occasionally imaginative, and affected toward standardization by the strong efforts of schools. But authentic and interesting as this language may be, it must be remembered that it exists, in *The Catcher in the Rye*, as only one part of an artistic achievement. The language was not written for itself, but as a part of a greater whole. Like the great Twain work with which it is often compared, a study of *The Catcher in the Rye* repays both the linguist and the literary critic; for as one critic has said, 'In them, 1884 and 1951 speak to us in the idiom and accent of two youthful travelers who have earned their passports to literary immortality.'

CLINTON W. TROWBRIDGE

The Symbolic Structure of The Catcher in the Rye

The symbolic content of Salinger's work has been hinted at, wildly and arbitrarily interpreted, overlooked, and even denied. In view of the fact that Salinger is the most self-conscious and deliberate of artists (it always surprises the undergraduate to learn that *The Catcher in the Rye* took ten years to write and was originally twice as long), as well as one whose interest in symbolism proclaims itself in the very title of his novel, it seems surprising that Salinger's use of symbolism has never been closely studied. In fiction, as in poetry, a symbol cannot be fully understood without discussing it in relation to the entire work. Yet it is just this that those critics who deal with Salinger's use of symbolism have failed to do. This lack has tended to make their remarks either tantalizing, absurd, or simply obtuse. For instance, the great significance that the Central Park ducks have for Holden Caulfield is hardly more than suggested in the following passage: "Like the Central Park ducks in winter, Holden is essentially homeless, frozen out." An example of the absurdities into which the arbitrary symbolmonger can be led is revealed in the following passage from Leslie Fiedler. Referring to *The Catcher in the Rye*, he writes: "It is the Orestes-Iphigenia story, we see there, that Salinger all along had been trying to rewrite, the account of a Fury-haunted brother redeemed by his priestess-sister; though Salinger demotes that sister in age, thus downgrading the tone of the legend from tragic to merely pathetic."

From *Sewanee Review* 74, no. 3 (July–September 1966). © 1966 The University of the South.

Only a complete failure to see what Salinger is trying to do in *The Catcher* can account for the obtuseness of this remark from another Salinger debunker, Maxwell Geismar: "For the later sections of the narrative are simply an episodic account of Holden Caulfield's 'lost weekend' in New York City which manages to sustain our interest but hardly deepens our understanding." Finally, another critic goes so far as to praise Salinger for not making use of symbolism. "In his work we find no showy or covert gesture in the direction of Symbolism."

As has been generally recognized, *The Catcher in the Rye* is the story of a quest, a search for truth in a world that has been dominated by falsity, the search for personal integrity by a hero who constantly falls short of his own ideal, who, in fact, participates in the very falsity he is trying to escape. The dramatic part of the novel stems from two things: that the hero's conflict is both internal and external and that it increases in intensity as his vision of inner and outer falsity becomes more and more overwhelming. What Fiedler calls "the pat Happy Ending" is simply the resolution of this conflict, a superbly appropriate one if we take into account what Salinger's intention is.

Thematically speaking, Salinger's intent is to present us with the plight of the idealist in the modern world. The undergraduate's, particularly the idealist undergraduate's, enthusiasm for *The Catcher* shows a recognition of this basic purpose as well as compliments Salinger's rendering of his theme. A college student writes: "Why do I like *The Catcher?* Because it puts forth in a fairly good argument the problems which boys of my age face, and also perhaps the inadequacy with which some of us cope with them. I have great admiration for Caulfield because he didn't compromise. . . . He likes the only things really worth liking, whereas most of us like all the things that aren't worth liking. Because he is sincere he won't settle for less."

The idealist, the person who sees a difference between what is and what ought to be and is bothered by that vision into some sort of action, has a number of alternatives facing him. If he is to remain an idealist, he must either strive to find his ideal world or attempt to reform what is into what ought to be. That is, his idealism can be either personal and escapist or impersonal and social. He can, of course, become disillusioned about the possibilities of attaining his end and, as a result, abandon, modify, or change his ideal.

What happens to Holden, and what constitutes, therefore, the structural pattern of the novel, is that, as a result of a frighteningly clear vision of the disparity between what is and what ought to be both in the world and in himself and because of an increasing feeling of incapacity to re-form either, he attempts to escape into a series of ideal worlds, fails, and is finally brought to the realization of a higher and more impersonal ideal, that man and the world, in spite of all their imperfections, are to be loved.

The first of the ideal worlds into which Holden tries to escape is the sophisticated, man-about-town's New York City, the symbol to virtually every New England prep school boy of the glamorous adult life that his school is the monastic and detested antithesis of. Although Holden is hardly in the right frame of mind to enjoy fully the anticipation of the typical prep school boy's dream—a long weekend on the town—and although he has even seen through this dream, his parting words: "Sleep tight, ya morons!" do represent a complete rejection of the adolescent world. The action that immediately follows reveals Holden trying to play the part of an adult. His first encounter, the scene with Mrs. Morrow, is, significantly enough, his most successful one. He is taken, delightfully, on his own terms. He is allowed to play the man-of-the-world, though only, it is evident, because he is so clearly *playing* it. The rest of his experiences as a man-of-the-world, until that image is destroyed by Maurice, are increasingly unsuccessful. It is his lack of sophistication rather than her unwillingness that is the reason for the failure of the Faith Cavendish affair, but he is refused a drink by the waiter and patronized as well as taken advantage of by the three "grools" from Seattle, screamed at by Horwitz the taxi driver, and treated very much as the younger brother by Lillian Simmons at Ernie's. During these scenes we learn more about Holden's real affections (his love for the childish innocence and simplicity of his sister and Jane Gallagher) and the degree of his detestation for the very part he is playing and the adult world that he believes insists on his playing that part. Then comes the climactic scene with Sunny and its devastating aftermath.

Maurice's question "Innarested in a little tail t'night?" constitutes a challenge to Holden's image of himself as a suave sophisticate and thus must be answered affirmatively. His subsequent failure with Sunny and the brutality of Maurice's treatment of him are forceful ways of destroying Holden's man-of-the-world image of himself. More important to us, however, is our learning at this point of the nature and degree of Holden's sexual and religious idealism. He cannot use people. Like Christ, he finds pity and compassion to be stronger in him than self-will; unlike Christ, he is unable to find anything in himself approximating to the love of God, anything that can make of this pity and compassion a positive force. And so Holden is merely depressed to the point of contemplating suicide. Already we have the suggestion of what is to become so important later in the novel, that since Holden cannot live up to his Christ ideal, he will choose to emulate the only other character in the Bible he likes, the lunatic that "lived in the tombs and kept cutting himself with stones". It is significant that just as Holden rejected the adolescent world in his parting shout to his dormitory mates at

Pencey Prep, so Sunny dismisses his pretensions of being an adult with the wonderfully casual, and completely devastating, "So long, crumb-bum."

His vision of himself as a man-of-the-world has not been completely destroyed however, merely altered to young man-of-the-world, a pose that he has tested before, that, in fact, he has just learned that he cannot emerge from. And so he calls up Sally Hayes and makes a date with her to go to a matinee. Sally Hayes represents the double nature of the social world as it is. It is full of falsity but undeniably attractive. "She gave me a pain in the ass, but she was very good-looking." She both dramatizes for us the appeal that social conformity has for Holden and shows us his weakness in failing to escape from it. She fits in beautifully with his genuine leather bags from Mark Cross, but we learn in this section of the novel that one of the things that most bothers Holden about things as they are is that appearances seem to have more power than reality. How much money you have, what your social position is, what your father does for a living, what church you belong to, even what you look like, all these things are superficialities that separate us from our fellow man, from ourselves, and ultimately from the life of integrity, from truth. Even the nuns, against whose genuine charity Holden so pitilessly contrasts the false philanthropy of Sally Hayes's mother, see things as Catholics; at least Holden thinks that they do. To Holden the adult world is dominated by categories, so much so that it can only be fled from. It is this vision that leads Holden to value the child over the adult (the child has not yet learned to experience the world in terms of categories) as well as to seek a personal escape from society.

Holden's dilemma, however, is that while he sees the phoniness of the world in which he lives, he is bound to that world through ties of affection as well as through force of habit and social pressure. Thus when he finally sees Sally Hayes, the "queen of the phonies", he says, "I felt like marrying her the minute I saw her. I'm crazy. I didn't even *like* her much, and yet all of a sudden I felt like I was in love with her and wanted to marry her. I swear to God I'm crazy. I admit it." When he proposes to Sally that they go off to New England together to live a *Farewell to Arms* sort of idyllic life, he is desperately trying to escape from the ever-encroaching adult world and at the same time carry off that which is attractive to him in it. But this is the sort of romantic escape that Holden rejects, though only after he has been rejected, and he ends by insulting and abandoning her, defeated once again in his quest for an ideal world. In abandoning Sally he has for the second time turned his back on himself as an adolescent. Now he tries again to become a man, this time by seeking advice from his former advisor at a previous school, Carl Luce.

In many ways Carl Luce represents the ideal of the man-about-town that Holden still dimly wants to become. He is several years older than

Holden and has all the appearances of the suave sophisticate. He has a Chinese mistress and seems to Holden to be cooly in control of his life. Yet his lack of understanding of Holden's plight and even more his lack of concern for it depresses Holden to the point where all he can do is sneak home and seek comfort in the company of the only person he knows will not disappoint him, his sister Phoebe. Luce's advice, that Holden needs to discover "the patterns of his mind", represents the idea of adjustment to the world as it is that is the dubious gift of psychoanalysis, and though only dimly understood as such by Holden, it is more a "cure" for idealism than a way of expressing it.

With Phoebe, Holden is at home in a world of innocence and integrity. He can trust her to take his side, to understand and sympathize. Thus it is doubly depressing when she reacts in just the opposite manner. Without even being told, she knows that he has been kicked out, and her "Oh, why did you *do* it?" affects him so deeply that he confesses far more than he intends to about the extent of his own nihilistic world-weariness. Phoebe's penetrating "You don't like *any*thing that's happening" forces him to make some sort of affirmation, to explain the sort of idealism that would justify so sad-making a picture of the world as it is. Neither his affirmation of his love of goodness (his brother Allie, James Castle) nor what might be called his love of pure being (just being with his sister) satisfies Phoebe, but Holden's memory of James Castle, the only person he has ever known who died for a principle, suggests to him a way in which he can devote his life to the protection of goodness. The significance of the catcher image lies in three things. First of all, it is a saviour image, and shows us the extent of Holden's religious idealism. Secondly, it crystallizes for us Holden's concept of good and evil; childhood is good, the only pure good, but it is surrounded by perils, the cliff of adolescence over which the children will plunge into the evil of adulthood unless stopped. But finally, the image is based on a misunderstanding. The Burns poem goes "If a body *meet a body*" not "if a body *catch a body*", and the fact that Phoebe is aware of this and Holden is not, plus the manner in which these two words ("catch" and "meet") are reexamined and re-interpreted by Holden at the end of the novel, shows us in a powerful and deeply suggestive way the center of Holden's difficulty. Both Holden's nihilistic view of life as it is and his notion of what life ought to be are based on a misunderstanding of man's place in the universe. In this central metaphor is condensed the essence of the novel, though not until the end does Holden fully understand the significance of the difference between "man catching" and "man meeting".

Of course, the catcher image does not represent a workable ideal, and Holden knows that. Its very impossibility means that all Holden is left with is his nihilism. He tells Phoebe that he plans to go out West and work on a ranch, but he shows that his real desire is to be saved from the emptiness of his negativism when he telephones Mr. Antolini and when he admits that he almost hopes that his parents will catch him as he sneaks out of the apartment. The catcher, in fact, wants to be caught, the saviour saved.

Mr. Antolini, a former English teacher of Holden's, is the nearest thing that Holden knows to the non-phony adult, and, as such, he is Holden's last refuge. As the person who protected the body of James Castle, he is also to Holden a kind of catcher figure, an image of his own ideal, therefore. In his understanding concern for Holden, and through his remarkably appropriate advice, Antolini does, in fact, seem to be saving him. Holden's physical relaxation, as well as the fact that he seems to have abandoned his plan to run off to the West (he even tells Antolini he plans to call up Jane Gallagher in the morning), augurs well for his spiritual recovery. What Antolini tells him, in essence, is that his presently depressed state is a perfectly natural result of an awareness of evil, the imperfectness of man and the world, and what he promises him is that if only he will not give up his quest for truth, he will find a way of incorporating his idealism about man and the world into some sort of action, some constructive way of life. His promise that a formal education will help him discover his potentialities—the ways in which he personally can contribute toward the implementation of the ideal—is what he means by discovering the "size [of one's] mind". The phrase, so close to Carl Luce's "the pattern of your mind", represents a wholly contrary idea. It is not adjustment to the world but adjustment to one's self that Mr. Antolini is advocating. With his quotations from Stekel, he is urging Holden toward maturity and a more practical and less egotistical idealism. But then all is ruined by what is basically Holden's intolerance of human imperfection. He is awakened by Antolini's patting him on the head, and once more he rejects what *is* because of its lack of perfection. Pursued by doubts about his interpretation of Antolini's apparent homosexuality as well as guilt feelings about his rejection of Antolini ("even if he was a flit he certainly'd been very nice to me"), he wanders in a state of terrible depression toward literal as well as figurative death.

The literal and figurative coalesce as Holden seems to be plunging into a void each time he crosses the street; he manages to get to the other side only by praying to his dead brother Allie to save him. So terrible is Holden's depression, so complete his sense of alienation from the world of the living, that in his disturbed imagination only the dead, idealized brother can save him from the nothingness, the hellish state of his own nihilism. Resting on a Fifth Avenue bench he comes to a vision of the only ideal world that now seems left to him. Though he does not believe in the serious possibility of the deaf-mute image of himself any more than he did of the catcher figure, it is equally significant as a metaphor of his state of mind. Just as in the catcher image Holden was showing his devotion to the Christ ideal, so in the deaf-mute figure Holden is revealing his allegiance to the only other character he likes in the Bible, the lunatic who lives in the tombs and cuts himself with stones. They are, of course, obverse images of each other: save the world or completely reject it, cherish and protect the good or wall yourself in from the evil, choose health and happiness or the masochistic lunacy of isolation and self-pity. Holden's disillusionment is complete, his search for truth apparently over. He has only to say good-bye to Phoebe and return to her the money she lent to him before he starts West. It is as if he was saying good-bye to life itself, a suggestion that Salinger enforces by having Holden almost killed as he runs across the street.

That Holden has given up his idealism, that his decision to go West represents not an escape into an ideal world, as he had formerly thought of it as being, but rather a rejection of his quest, is made clear to us in the next section of the novel. Throughout the novel Holden has been in search of a world, a way of life, an ideal that does not change. What he has never been able to accept is the mutability of life. The images that he loves are static images: Jane Gallagher as the girl who keeps her kings in the back row; children who, because of their absorption in the present and because of their innocence, seem to be unchanging; and above all (and increasingly as the novel progresses) the world of the dead: the martyred James Castle, the idealized, dead younger brother Allie, the natural history museum where even the smells are the same year after year. Holden's absorption with the idea of death reaches its culmination, appropriately enough, in the Egyptian tombs of the Museum of Art. The marvel of the Egyptians was that they were able to achieve permanence with something as essentially impermanent as the human body. The mummies represent the kind of conquest over time and mutability that Holden has been in search of all along. While to the younger boys that Holden is guiding, the tombs are spooky places from which they soon flee, to Holden they are symbolic of the peace and permanence that he so desperately wants. What he discovers there, in the form of the obscenity written under one of the glass cases, is that the quest for permanence is a hopeless one. "That's the whole trouble. You can't ever find a place that's nice and peaceful, because there isn't any." Even death is no escape. The trip West is embraced, but without the usual Caulfield enthusiasm, as a sort of negative ideal. It is the most pathetic, as well as the most fantastic, image of himself that Holden has yet created; and we see how little he is really interested in it, how sadly he must in fact be contemplating it, in the next scene when Phoebe arrives and insists on going with him.

The brilliance of the concluding section of the novel lies almost wholly in its irony. The ironic pattern has already been established that each time one of Holden's ideal images of himself is tested by reality it fails and in so failing shows us the phoniness of that particular image. But the images of himself that have been tested thus far have been phony ones and we have been relieved rather than disappointed that he has failed to act in accordance with them. Consider, for example, his behavior with Sunny. Here, for the first time, however, an apparently genuine image of himself is being tested: Holden the non-phony, the only non-phony left, at least in the adult world, is going to preserve his own integrity by keeping himself unspotted from the world and at the same time provide an oasis in the desert of phoniness for those who are worth of salvation, mainly Phoebe and his older brother D. B. There are remnants of the catcher image in this picture of himself but more significant is the world-weariness, the alienation of himself from all but a chosen few, his apparent contempt for and hatred of the world.

But this too, when tested, turns out to be a phony image of himself. His refusal to allow Phoebe to accompany him, his anger with her for even wanting to go, provides us, and finally himself, with a climatic insight into his real character. In the first place, he is by no means as alienated from his world as he or we supposed. We have believed the theatre to be the epitome of phoniness to Holden; yet what most infuriated Holden about Phoebe's decision to leave with him is that she will not be acting in her school-play if she does. And consider the ironies involved in the fact that the part she is to play is that of Benedict Arnold. He is concerned over whether or not she has had lunch. He tells her that she *has* to go back to school. In fact, we see quite clearly that she is now behaving like him, has taken on his role. This vision of himself, as well as his sudden realization of the extent to which he has endangered the very goodness and innocence that he most wanted to protect, so horrifies him that he immediately abandons his plan to go West, tells her he is going home instead, and carefully and touchingly tries to lead her back to normalcy. Holden, who has apparently been uninfluenced by the various people who have tried to help him in the course of the novel, acts in this scene like a combination of Mr. Spencer, Antolini, and Phoebe as she had been on the previous night. What he tells her even smacks of his headmaster's statement, so abhorred by Holden at the time, that life's a game and has to be played according to the rules.

Secondly, Holden's behavior with Phoebe proves to us the genuineness of the catcher image. When tested, his love for Phoebe and his desire to save her innocence is far greater than his hatred for the world and his determination to abandon it. His love of good is stronger than his hatred of evil. And so, paradoxically, he is saved through saving; the catcher is caught by the person he most wants to catch. Of course, Holden is by no means completely saved, merely reclaimed from the death-like state of his world-weariness. He does, after all, suffer a nervous breakdown. He doesn't know if he's going to "apply himself" or not. Though the conclusion of the novel is hardly a "pat Happy Ending", then, it is affirmative; for Holden has caught some glimpse of how he can implement the catcher image of himself in action and as a result embraces a higher and more impersonal ideal: that man and the world are to be loved in spite of their imperfections.

The experience that leads Holden to this final affirmation occurs while he is watching Phoebe ride the carousel in the zoo.

> All the kids kept trying to grab for the gold ring, and so was old Phoebe, and I was sort of afraid she'd fall off the goddam horse, but I didn't say anything or do anything. The thing with kids is, if they want to grab for the gold ring, you have to let them do it, and not say anything. If they fall off, they fall off, but it's bad if you say anything to them.

Understood in terms of its connection with the original catcher metaphor, what Holden is saying is something like this: innocence and goodness, epitomized in the condition of the child, are not static conditions; just as the child must grow up through adolescence into adulthood, so must innocence and goodness risk this passage through experience and evil. One cannot push the metaphor too far, but the gold ring suggests the promise of life, the beatific end that is the prize as well as the goal. Some are defeated by experience and evil—fall off the horse; others never get the gold ring—fail to attain the promise of life. The important thing to realize is that these are the conditions of life and that (to put it back in terms of the catcher metaphor), rather than to attempt the impossible (catch and hold something that by its very nature cannot be caught and held—childhood, innocence), man should meet man, form a relationship of love and understanding with him, and in so doing help him toward his goal just as Holden is doing here with Phoebe. Man cannot save the world; he should not despise it; he may, however, love it. The effects on Holden are immediate.

> I was damn near bawling, I felt so damn happy, if you want to know the truth. I don't know why. It was just that she looked so damn *nice*, the way she kept going around and around, in her blue coat and all. God, I wish you could've been there.

This final sentence sets the tone for the concluding chapter and shows the effect on Holden of his altered catcher ideal. He misses everybody, even Maurice. The concern to communicate, to establish a relationship with man, has led to the love of man. Holden, whose actions and ideas had been prompted largely by his supersensitivity to evil, is now so sensitive to good that he can even love Maurice.

JAMES BRYAN

The Psychological Structure of The Catcher in the Rye

Standing by the "crazy cannon" on Thomsen Hill one sunless afternoon, listening to the cheers from a football game below, "the two teams bashing each other all over the place," Holden Caulfield tries to "feel some kind of a good-by" to the prep school he has just flunked out of:

> I was lucky. All of a sudden I thought of something that helped make me know I was getting the hell out. I suddenly remembered this time, in around October, that I and Robert Tichener and Paul Campbell were chucking a football around, in front of the academic building. They were nice guys, especially Tichener. It was just before dinner and it was getting pretty dark out, but we kept chucking the ball around anyway. It kept getting darker and darker, and we could hardly *see* the ball anymore, but we didn't want to stop doing what we were doing. Finally we had to. This teacher that taught biology, Mr. Zambesi, stuck his head out of this window in the academic building and told us to go back to the dorm and get ready for dinner. If I get a chance to remember that kind of stuff, I can get a good-by when I need one.

From *PMLA* 89, no. 5 (October 1974). © 1974 The Modern Language Association of America.

A careful look at this first scene in the novel provides clues for interpretation, by no means crucial in themselves, but illustrative of a pattern of scene construction and suggestive imagery which does yield meaning. Appropriate is this adolescent's sense of his "darkling plain" where, if an extravagant metaphor be allowed, "ignorant football teams clash by afternoon." In a pattern repeated throughout the novel, he thinks back to a time when he and two "nice guys" passed a football around, shared rather than fought over it, though even then the idyllic state seemed doomed. Holden is poised between two worlds, one he cannot return to and one he fears to enter, while the image of a football conflict is probably an ironic commentary on Holden's adolescence, football's being a civilized ritualization of human aggression.

What is forcing Holden's crisis? Everything in the idyllic scene points to the encroachment of time—the season, the time of day, even such verbal echoes from his friends' names as "ticking," "bell," and "pall." Accrual of this sort of evidence will justify what may seem overinterpretation here, especially of the significance of a biology teacher's ending the boys' innocent pleasures—their idyll already sentenced by time, darkness. More than anything else Holden fears the biological imperatives of adulthood—sex, senescence, and death—which are delicately foreshadowed in the innocent October scene by the unwelcome call to dinner.

Much of the *Catcher* criticism has testified to Holden's acute moral and esthetic perceptions—his eye for beauty as well as "phoniness"—but the significance of his immaturity in intensifying these perceptions has not been sufficiently stressed nor explained. Precisely because this sixteen-year-old acts "like I'm about thirteen" and even "like I was only about twelve," he is hypersensitive to the exploitations and insensitivity of the post-pubescent world and to the fragile innocence of children. A central rhythm of the narrative has Holden confronting adult callousness and retreating reflexively into thoughts and fantasies about children, childlike Jane Gallaghers, and especially his ten-year-old sister, Phoebe. These juxtapositions render both worlds more intensely and at the same time qualify Holden's judgments by showing that they are emotionally—or, as we shall see, neurotically—induced.

While a fair number of critics have referred to Holden's "neurosis," none has accepted Salinger's invitation—proffered in the form of several key references to psychoanalysis—to participate in a full-fledged psychoanalytical reading. The narrative, after all, was written in a mental hospital with Holden under the care of a "psychoanalyst guy." One problem is that Holden tells us very little about "what my lousy childhood was like" or the event that may have brought on the trauma behind all of his problems: the death of a younger brother when Holden was thirteen. We know little more than that the family has been generally disrupted since and that Holden has not come to grips with life as he should have. Allie's death takes place outside the province of the narrative, but a valuable psychological study might still be made of the progression of Holden's breakdown—how he provokes fights in which he will be beaten, makes sexual advances which he cannot carry through, and unconsciously alienates himself from many of the people he encounters. As a step toward psychological understanding, I shall consider certain manifestations of Holden's disturbances. An examination of the structure, scene construction, and suggestive imagery reveals a pattern of agression and regression, largely sexual, which is suggested in the Pencey Prep section, acted out in the central part of the novel, and brought to a curious climax in the Phoebe chapters.

I

One implication of the novel's main motif, that which polarizes childlike and adult responses, concerns the dilemma of impossible alternatives. Here characters suggest human conditions that Holden either cannot or must not make his own. In the novel's first paragraph Holden tells us that his brother D. B. has "prostituted" his writing talents by going to Hollywood—a failure implicitly contrasted throughout with the purity of Allie, the brother who died before the temptations of adulthood. Holden's first encounter is with Spencer, the old teacher who fills his mind with thoughts of age and death, while his last is with Phoebe, his emblem of unattainable childhood beauty. Stradlater and Ackley are antithetically placed to represent what Holden fears he may become if he is either sexually appropriative or repressed. Because the novel is built around these impossible alternatives, because Holden's world provides no one he can truly emulate, the many critics who read *Catcher* as a sweeping indictment of society have virtually drowned out those who attack Holden's immaturity. One feels the justice of this, yet the novel's resolution, like all of Salinger's mature fiction, transcends sociological indictment in affirming individual responsibility. When Holden answers for his own life as he verges toward some rather dreadful appropriation of his own, he begins to come to terms at once with himself and society.

At the outset of traditional quest narratives, the hero often receives sage advice from a wise old man or crone. The best old Spencer can do is to wish Holden a depressing "good luck," just as another agent of education, a woman "around a hundred years old," will do in the penultimate chapter. Spencer's plaintive "I'm trying to *help* you, if I can" and the old woman's irrelevant chatter near the end bracket the bulk of the narrative in which Holden seeks answers from without. And in both scenes the human resources that do see him through are dramatized in his compassion for the two old people.

Though the Spencer chapter serves notice that Holden has flunked the administrative requirements of education, we learn immediately that he draws sustenance from art. He returns to his room to reread in Isak Dinesen's *Out of Africa* that chronicle of sensitivity surrounded by primitive id forces. At this point he is interrupted by eighteen-year-old Robert Ackley, a grotesque possibility of what Holden may become if his manhood is similarly thwarted. Unleavened sensitivity will not be enough as we see Holden vacillating through five chapters between Ackley and Ward Stradlater, the equally unacceptable model of male aggressiveness. Stradlater's vitality is dramatized in his "Year Book" handsomeness, "damn good build," and superior strength, while Ackley's impotence is reflected in acned, unsightly looks, general enervation, and repulsive habits. Stradlater is slovenly too—Holden calls him a "secret slob"—but he elicits some admiration where Ackley is only pathetic.

Stradlater's date for the evening is Jane Gallagher, a girl with whom Holden has had a summer romance. That relationship was characterized by Jane's habit of keeping her kings in the back row when they played checkers—later on, Holden says specifically that their lovemaking never went beyond the handholding stage. In Holden's request that Stradlater ask Jane if she still keeps her kings in the back row, one critic sees Holden signaling warnings about her "sexy" date. Holden tells us in another chapter that Jane was the kind of girl you never wanted to "kid too much." "I think I really like it best," he goes on to say,

> when you can kid the pants off a girl when the opportunity arises, but it's a funny thing. The girls I like best are the ones I never feel much like kidding. Sometimes I think they'd *like* it if you kidded them—in fact, I *know* they would—but it's hard to get started, once you've known them a pretty long time and never kidded them.

On an action level, of course, Jane did keep her kings in the back row and Holden is indeed talking about kidding. But such double entendres as "kidding the pants off a girl" reveal not only Holden's sexual preoccupations but the elaborate coding his mind has set up against recognizing such preoccupations for what they are. In the early parts of the novel, Salinger may be training the reader to see through Holden's words in these rather apparent ways, thus to prepare for the most subtle and crucial coding of all in the Phoebe section.

Stradlater's strength and sexuality cause Holden to discountenance his own. This night, for example, Stradlater uses Holden's "Vitalis" hair tonic and borrows his "hound's-tooth" jacket, leaving Holden "so nervous I nearly went crazy" as he thinks of this "sexy bastard" with Jane. Conversely, Holden this same night endures Ackley's droning narrative of his sexual exploits with a final comment, "He was a virgin if I ever saw one. I doubt if he ever even gave anybody a feel." Not until Holden faces the Ackley and Stradlater in himself will he be able to do the purgative writing that is of course the form of the novel itself. They are almost like doppelgangers; one will interrupt him when he reads to escape while the other rejects the composition he ghostwrites because it is escapist. Even when he attacks the cocksure Stradlater after the latter's date with Jane, Holden's brief blood initiation is, as we shall see, a needful battle against himself. Right after the fight, getting no consolation from that other polar figure, Ackley, Holden leaves Pencey Prep.

The five Stradlater and Ackley chapters make for closely woven, dramatized exposition of Holden's psychological quandary which prepares for the loose, episodic middle section of the novel where Holden goes questing after experience and wisdom. Rejecting the alternatives implicit in Stradlater and Ackley, Holden wants his life to be vital without appropriation, innocent without retrogression. In the Phoebe section where the novel tightens up again, we shall see that Holden nearly becomes *both* appropriative and retrogressive and that it is precisely Holden's awareness of this that points the way to maturity.

Immediately after arriving in New York and checking into a hotel room, Holden is treated to a fresh installment of the Ackley-Stradlater antithesis. Through one window across an airshaft he sees a transvestite dress himself and mince before a mirror, while in the window above a couple squirt water "out of their mouths at each other." Holden confesses at this point that "In my *mind*, I'm probably the biggest sex maniac you ever saw" and that he might enjoy such "crumby stuff" as squirting water in a girl's face. Characteristically, he decides to call his chaste Jane, thinks better of it, and phones Faith Cavendish, a stripper recommended to Holden as one who "didn't mind doing it once in a while." Her ritual objections to the late-hour call dispensed with, she suggests a meeting the next day. Holden declines, however, and "damn near" gives his "kid sister Phoebe a buzz," justifying the switch by describing Phoebe's charms at length. Later in a bar he is flanked on his left by "this funny-looking guy" nervously reciting to his date "every single goddam play" of a football game he had seen, and on the other side by a suave young man giving a beautiful girl "a feel under the table," over her embarassed objections, "at the same time telling her all about some guy in his dorm that had . . . nearly commited suicide." All around him Holden sees distorted reflections of his own spasmodic aggression and withdrawal. And in the last instance cited we get an early hint of one of the most dangerous manifestations of his neurosis: his association of sex with death.

When he retreats in a panic to Grand Central Station, for example, he begins to read a discarded magazine to "make me stop thinking" about Antolini's apparent homosexual advances. One article convinces him that his hormones are "lousy" and another that he would "be dead in a couple of months" from cancer. What seems burlesque here ("That magazine was some little cheerer upper") becomes urgent in Holden's response to an obscene legend he sees shortly after in Phoebe's school:

> Somebody'd written "Fuck you" on the wall. It drove me damn near crazy. I thought how Phoebe and all the other little kids would see it, and how they'd wonder what the hell it meant, and then finally some dirty kid would tell them—all cockeyed, naturally—what it meant. . . . I figured it was some perverty bum that'd sneaked in the school late at night to take a leak or something and then wrote it on the wall. I kept picturing myself catching him at it, and how I'd smash his head on the stone steps till he was good and goddam dead and bloody. But I knew, too, I wouldn't have the guts to do it. I knew that. That made me even more depressed. I hardly even had the guts to rub it off the wall with my *hand*, if you want to know the truth. I was afraid some teacher would catch me rubbing it off and would think *I'd* written it. But I rubbed it out anyway, finally.

As we shall see, Holden is more repelled by the "obscenity" of the sexual act itself than by the obscene word. And his fear of being identified with the sort of "pervert" who planted it in Phoebe's school is reiterated when, in one more withdrawal, he goes to the mummy tomb in the museum and again finds the legend. At this point he decides,

> You can't ever find a place that's nice and peaceful, because there isn't any. You may *think* there is, but once you get there, when you're not looking, somebody'll sneak up and write "Fuck you" right under your nose. Try it sometime. I think, even, if I ever die, and they stick me in a cemetery, and I have a tombstone and all, it'll say "Holden Caulfield" on it, and then what year I was born and what year I died, and right under that it'll say "Fuck you." I'm positive, in fact.

It is not enough to leave it that Holden's sickness has brought about this odd commingling of lovemaking and dying in his mind. Looking back at Holden's ostensibly random comments on various fascinations and aversions, one sees a subtle but coherent psychological pattern taking shape. Early in the novel we learn of his interest in Egyptian mummification and his particular fascination—mentioned again in the tomb scene—that the process ensured that "their faces wouldn't rot or anything." After watching the "perverts" squirt water in each other's faces, Holden reflects that

> if you don't really like a girl, you shouldn't horse around with her at all, and if you *do* like her, then you're supposed to like her face, and if you like her face, you ought to be careful about doing crumby stuff to it, like squirting water all over it.

If there are sexual inhibitions reflected in Holden's curious concern with the "preservation of faces," they must also be implicit in his general and constant longing for a state of changelessness. He laments, for instance, that though his beloved museum never changed, he did:

> The best thing, though, in that museum was that everything always stayed right where it was. Nobody'd move. You could go there a hundred thousand times, and that Eskimo would still be just finished catching those two fish, the birds would still be on their way south. . . . Nobody'd be different. The only thing that would be different would be *you*. Not that you'd be so much older or anything. It wouldn't be that, exactly. You'd just be different, that's all. You'd have an overcoat on this time. . . . Or you'd heard your mother and father having a terrific fight in the bathroom. . . . I can't explain what I mean. And even if I could, I'm not sure I'd feel like it.

Readers experienced in the strategies of unreliable narration will suspect that Holden probably does somehow "explain" and that there must be a reason why he's not sure he'd "feel like it" if he could. One notices, as a possible clue, that the museum is associated here and elsewhere with Phoebe.

> I kept thinking about old Phoebe going to that museum on Saturdays the way I used to. I thought how she'd see the same stuff I used to see, and how *she'd* be different every time she saw

it. It didn't exactly depress me to think about it, but it didn't make me feel gay as hell, either. Certain things should stay the way they are. . . . I know that's impossible, but it's too bad anyway.

Indeed, Holden's feelings about Phoebe may explain much that is puzzling in his narrative.

II

The expository sections of the novel dramatize Holden's problems as essentially sexual and moral. Yet most critical readings of the novel's ending either ignore those things or imply their absence by declaring that the resolution is "blunted" or else "humanly satisfying" while "artistically weak." Those critics who attest to a harmonious resolution generally do so on philosophical grounds, the effect being a divorce of theme from Holden's human situation. To deny a fused sexual and moral resolution of some sort in the closing emotional crescendo of the Phoebe section would, it seems to me, impugn the integrity of the novel.

I am suggesting that the urgency of Holden's compulsions, his messianic desire to guard innocence against adult corruption, for example, comes of a frantic need to save his sister from himself. It may be Phoebe's face that Holden unconsciously fears may be desecrated; hence the desire to protect Phoebe's face that compels his fascination with mummification. And it may be Phoebe who provokes his longing for stasis because he fears that she may be changed—perhaps at his own hand. Holden's association of sex with death surely points to some sexual guilt—possibly the fear that he or Phoebe or both may "die" if repressed desires are acted out.

I do not mean to imply that Holden's desires, if they are what I suggest, drive him inexorably to Phoebe's bed. The psychoanalytical axiom may here apply that a sister is often the first replacement of a mother as love object, and that normal maturation guides the boy from sister to other women. At this point in his life, Holden's sexuality is swaying precariously between reversion and maturation—a condition structurally dramatized throughout and alluded to in this early description:

I was sixteen then, and I'm seventeen now, and sometimes I act like I'm about thirteen. It's really ironical, because I'm six foot two and a half and I have gray hair. I really do. The one side of my head—the right side—is full of millions of gray hairs. I've had them since I was a kid. And yet I still act sometimes like I was only about twelve. Everybody says that, especially my father. It's partly true, but it isn't *all* true. . . . Sometimes I act a lot older than I am—I really do—but people never notice it.

The narrator's overall perspective is thus mapped out: his present age representing some measure of maturity, and thirteen and twelve the vacillation that normally comes at puberty and that is so much more painful when it occurs as late as sixteen. This vacillation is somehow resolved in a climax beginning in Phoebe's bedroom (or rather the bedroom of D. B., the corrupt brother, where she sleeps) and ending at the carrousel after Holden has refused to let her run away with him. However one interprets the ending, it comes as a surprise which is dramatically appropriate precisely because it shocks Holden. Hence, also, the aptness of providing only scattered hints of things to come through the quest section, hints which, in my presentation, will necessarily seem tentative.

One notes in passing, for example, Holden's sudden infatuation with Bernice, one of the prosaic Seattle girls, while they are dancing. "You really can dance," he tells her. "I have a kid sister that's only in the goddam fourth grade. You're about as good as she is, and she can dance better than anybody living or dead." A possible association might be made of the name of the young prostitute, "Sunny," with "Phoebe." Certainly Sunny's childlike aspects are emphasized throughout the episode:

> She was a pretty spooky kid. Even with that little bitty voice she had, she could sort of scare you a little bit. If she'd been a big old prostitute, with a lot of makeup on her face and all, she wouldn't have been half as spooky.

Holden has to beg off with the excuse that "I was a little premature in my calculations." His beating at the hands of Maurice, her pimp, suggests psychic punishment as well, particularly when Holden imagines that he's dying and pretends "I have a bullet in my gut."

More can be made of an assertion Holden is constrained to repeat that Phoebe is "too affectionate." After retreating from making the date with Faith, he describes Phoebe at length and tells the reader,

> She's all right. You'd like her. The only trouble is, she's a little too affectionate sometimes. She's very emotional, for a child. She really is.

Later, when Holden awakens Phoebe and "She put her arms around my neck and all," he blurts out:

> She's very affectionate. I mean she's quite affectionate, for a child. Sometimes she's even *too* affectionate. I sort of gave her a kiss.

One begins to recognize the brilliant stratagem of imprecise adolescent qualifiers such as "sort of," "I mean," "and all," and the nervous repetition of "affectionate" which dramatize Holden's confusion of restraint and desire. This confusion develops in the first passage as language moves from firm declaration to qualification; in the second, Phoebe's prescence provokes even more qualified language.

Then, there is the curious matter of "Little Shirley Beans," the record Holden buys for Phoebe:

> It was about a little kid that wouldn't go out of the house because two of her front teeth were out and she was ashamed to. . . . I knew it would knock old Phoebe out. . . . It was a very old, terrific record that this colored girl, Estelle Fletcher, made about twenty years ago. She sings it very Dixieland and whorehouse, and it doesn't sound at all mushy. If a white girl was singing it, she'd make it sound *cute* as hell, but old Estelle Fletcher knew what the hell she was doing, and it was one of the best records I ever heard.

The significance of the record is underscored by Holden's anxiousness to give it to Phoebe and his inordinate dismay when he breaks it:

> Then something terrible happened just as I got in the park. I dropped old Phoebe's record. It broke into about fifty pieces. . . . I damn near cried, it made me feel so terrible, but all I did was, I took the pieces out of the envelope and put them in my coat pocket.

One wonders if the accident wasn't psychically determined. If the Shirley Beans affair were a subject of dream analysis, the missing teeth, the shame, and the translation through "whorehouse" jazz by a singer who "knew what the hell she was doing" would conventionally suggest the loss of virginity. Hence, Holden's unconscious forces would dictate the destruction of this "record" as well as its purchase. In the same vein is the information Holden passes on, as he sneaks into the apartment to see Phoebe, that the maid wouldn't hear "because she had only one eardrum. She had this brother that stuck a straw down her ear when she was a kid, she once told me."

At one point Holden hears a child singing the song that becomes the anthem of his savior fantasies: "If a body catch a body coming through the rye." Yet in the next paragraph he buys the "Little Shirley Beans" record—the pairing symbolically dramatizes his conflict of protecting and of violating. His thoughts turn to the Olivier *Hamlet* he and Phoebe had watched and he singles out this highly suggestive scene:

> The best part in the whole picture was when old Ophelia's brother—the one that gets in the duel with Hamlet at the very end—was going away and his father was giving him a lot of advice. While the father kept giving him a lot of advice, old Ophelia was sort of horsing around with her brother, taking his dagger out of the holster, and teasing him and all while he was trying to look interested in the bull his father was shooting. That was nice. I got a big bang out of that. But you don't see that kind of stuff much. The only thing old Phoebe liked was when Hamlet patted this dog on the head.

In all of these early clues, one notices that the nearer Holden's desires come to surfacing, the more hesitant his language and behavior become. When the dreadful suggestions have the protective coloration of, say, the art of "Little Shirley Beans" or *Hamlet*, he is not so uneasy: "That was nice. I got a big bang out of that."

After a series of abortive adventures with women, Holden rather desperately seeks the counsel of a former classmate who was regarded as the dormitory's resident expert on sexual matters. Luce is too pompous to help, but his cutting assessments are probably accurate. He tells Holden that his "mind is immature" and recommends psychoanalysis, as he had done the last time they had talked. Holden's self-diagnosis at this point—that his "trouble" is an inability to get "sexy—I mean really sexy—with a girl I don't like a lot"—raises questions when one recalls his fraternal affection for Jane Gallagher and the relatively sexy episodes with the likes of Sally Hayes and "a terrible phony named Anne Louise Sherman." A probable answer, as we shall see, lies in his confused feelings about Phoebe.

All chances for normal sexual expression or even sexual understanding now depleted, Holden gets drunk and goes to Central Park to find "where the ducks go in winter." One critic reads this episode, filled as it is with thoughts of death, as Holden's "dark night of the soul," after which the boy begins to gain in psychic strength. It ought to be pointed out that Holden's breakdown occurs after the events of the narrative. His desperation in the park is certainly one extreme of his vacillation, the withdrawing extreme which is imaged by coldness and thoughts of death. Finally, he decides to see Phoebe, "in case I died and all," more explicitly associating Phoebe with death.

Holden makes his way into the apartment furtively—ostensibly to keep his parents from learning that he had flunked out of school. Yet his guilt seems obsessive. "I really should've been a crook," he says after telling the elevator operator that he was visiting the "Dicksteins" who live next door, that he has to wait for them in the hallway because he has a "bad leg," causing him to limp "like a bastard." Though his mother "has ears like a goddam bloodhound," his parents are out and he enters Phoebe's room undetected. Phoebe is asleep:

> She had her mouth way open. It's funny. You take adults, they look lousy when they're asleep and they have their mouths way open, but kids don't. Kids look all right. They can even have spit all over the pillow and they still look all right.

Suddenly Holden feels "swell" as he notices such things as Phoebe's discarded clothing arranged neatly on a chair. Throughout the Phoebe section, double entendres and sexually suggestive images and gestures multiply, most flowing naturally from Holden's mind while others, once the coding is perceived, become mechanical pointers to the psychological plot.

When Holden awakens Phoebe and is embarrassed by her overaffection, she eagerly tells him about the play in which she is "Benedict Arnold":

> "It starts out when I'm dying. This ghost comes in on Christmas Eve and asks me if I'm ashamed and everything. . . . Are you coming to it?"

When the Benedict Arnold image recurs at the end, we shall see that the role of "traitor" is precisely the one she must play if her brother is to weather his crisis. Phoebe then tells him about *The Doctor*, a movie she has seen "at the Lister Foundation" about "this doctor . . . that sticks a blanket over this child's face that's a cripple and can't walk. . . . and makes her suffocate. Then they make him go to jail for life imprisonment, but this child that he stuck the blanket over its head comes to visit him all the time and thanks him for what he did. He was a mercy killer."

This suggestive plot points to a horrible psychological possibility for Holden. He may "kill" Phoebe, pay his penalty agreeably, and even receive the gratitude of his victim. If interpretation here seems hard to justify, especially the implications of *Phoebe's* having suggested all this to Holden, consider the climax of the chapter in which Phoebe puts "the goddam pillow over her head" and refuses to come out. "She does that quite frequently," Holden reassures us—and then takes it all back: "She's a true madman sometimes." However innocent, Phoebe's responses to Holden's secret needs become the cataclyst for both his breakdown and recovery.

Through the next chapter Phoebe hears Holden out on his "categorial aversions," in Salinger's phrase, to all the "phoniness" that has soured his world. The conversation begins in a curious manner:

Then, just for the hell of it, I gave her a pinch on the behind. It was sticking way out in the breeze, the way she was laying on her side. She has hardly any behind. I didn't do it hard, but she tried to hit my hand anyway, but she missed.

Then all of a sudden, she said, "Oh, why did you *do* it?" She meant why did I get the axe again. It made me sort of sad, the way she said it.

Holden spells out his dissatisfactions at length—and indeed he cites valid and depressing instances of human failings—until Phoebe challenges him several times, "You don't like *anything* that's happening." "Name one thing," she demands. "One thing? One thing I like?" Holden replies. "Okay." At this point he finds he can't "concentrate too hot."

She was in a cockeyed position way the hell over the other side of the bed. She was about a thousand miles away.

He can't concentrate, I suggest, because the truth is too close.

About all I could think about were those two nuns that went around collecting dough in those beat-up old straw baskets.

Especially the one with the glasses with those iron rims. And
this boy I knew at Elkton Hills.

Repression has transferred the true thing he "likes a lot" to a nun, an
inviolable "sister," who, we remember, had embarrassed Holden by talking
about *Romeo and Juliet*, "that play [that] gets pretty sexy in parts." It may
also be significant that *Romeo and Juliet* involves forbidden love that ends
tragically—especially significant in connection with the other "thing"
Holden thinks about, James Castle, the boy who had killed himself wearing
Holden's turtleneck sweater.
     None of this will do for Phoebe and she repeats the challenge:

> "I like Allie," I said. "And I like doing what I'm doing right
> now. Sitting here with you, and talking, and thinking about
> stuff, and—"

When she objects that "Allie's dead," Holden tries to explain but gives up:

> "Anyway, I like it now," I said. "I mean right now. Sitting here
> with you and just chewing the fat and horsing—"

Her insistence drives him to the loveliest—and most sinister—fantasy in the
novel:

> "You know that song 'If a body catch a body comin' through
> the rye'? I'd like—"
>   "It's 'If a body *meet* a body coming through the rye!'" old
> Phoebe said.

Holden proceeds to conjure up the daydream of himself as catcher in the rye,
the protector of childhood innocence. As Phoebe implies, however, the song
is about romance, not romanticism. Because he has to, Holden has
substituted a messianic motive for the true, erotic one.
     In the next chapter Holden and Phoebe seem to be acting out a mock
romance, much the way Seymour Glass does with the little girl in "A
Perfect Day for Bananafish." The episode is at once movingly tender and
ominous. Holden finds Phoebe "sitting smack in the middle of the bed,
outside the covers, with her legs folded like one of those Yogi guys"—an
image one critic interprets as making her an emblem of "the still,

contemplative center of life." This may be valid for one level of Holden's mind. When he immediately asks her to dance, however, and "She practically jumped off the bed, and then waited while I took my shoes off," his excessive justification points to guilt:

> I don't like people that dance with little kids. . . . Usually they keep yanking the kid's dress up in the back by mistake, and the kid can't dance worth a damn *any*way, and it looks terrible, but I don't do it out in public with Phoebe or anything. We just horse around in the house. It's different with her anyway, because she can *dance*. She can follow anything you do. I mean if you hold her in close as hell so that it doesn't matter that your legs are so much longer. She stays right with you.

After the dance, Phoebe "jumped back in bed and got under the covers" and Holden "sat down next to her on the bed again . . . sort of out of breath." "'Feel my forehead,' she said all of a sudden." Phoebe claims she has learned to induce fever psychomatically so that

> "your whole forehead gets so hot you can burn somebody's hand."
>   That killed me. I pulled my hand away from her forehead, like I was in terrific danger. "Thanks for *tell*ing me," I said.
>   "Oh, I wouldn't've burned *your* hand. I'd've stopped before it got too—*Shhh!*" Then, quick as hell, she sat way the hell up in bed.

The parents have returned and the scene that follows, Holden gathering up his shoes and hiding in the closet as the mother interrogates Phoebe about the (cigarette) "smoke" in the bedroom and asks "were you warm enough?" is reminiscent of nothing so much as that mainstay of French farce, the lover hiding in the closet or under the bed as the girl ironically "explains" to husband or parent. More important are the implications of Phoebe's "heat." Though she cannot really induce it, her innocent compliance in the whole sexual charade does place Holden "in terrific danger."

When the mother leaves, Holden emerges from his hiding place and borrows money from Phoebe. Phoebe insists that he take all of her money and Holden "all of a sudden" begins to cry:

I couldn't help it. I did it so nobody could hear me, but I did it. It scared hell out of old Phoebe when I started doing it, and she came over and tried to make me stop, but once you get started, you can't just stop on a goddam *dime*. I was still sitting on the edge of the bed when I did it, and she put her old arm around my neck, and I put my arm around her, too, but I still couldn't stop for a long time. I thought I was going to choke to death or something. Boy, I scared hell out of poor old Phoebe. The damn window was open and everything, and I could feel her shivering and all, because all she had on was her pajamas. I tried to make her get back in bed, but she wouldn't go.

Holden's breakdown, his visiting of his own suffering on the child, the chill air, and the innocence of their intimacy in this moving scene signal his growing, frightening awareness of the other sort of intimacy. From now until he sees Phoebe again, Holden is in full flight. Nonetheless, their parting is filled with suggestions of a sort one might expect after a casual, normal sexual encounter. (The emphases in the following passage are my own.)

Then I *finished buttoning* my coat and all. I told her I'd *keep in touch with her*. She said *I could sleep with her* if I wanted to, but I said no, that I'd better beat it. . . . Then I took my hunting hat out of my pocket and *gave it to her*. She likes those kind of crazy hats. She didn't want to take it, but *I made her*. I'll bet she *slept with it* on. She really likes those kinds of hats. Then I told her again I'd *give her a buzz* if I got a chance, and then I left.

It is almost as if Holden is acknowledging the real content of the sexual charade and escaping while he can. It would also seem that realization, however vague, is equated with deed as Holden immediately indicates that he wanted to be punished:

It was a helluva lot easier getting out of the house than it was getting in, for some reason. For one thing, I didn't give much of a damn anymore if they caught me. I really didn't. I figured if they caught me, they caught me. I almost wished they did, in a way.

Holden leaves Phoebe to spend the night with Mr. Antolini, a former teacher who during the course of the evening offers sound if stilted assessments of Holden's future which become particularly relevant in the epilogue. Antolini has been drinking, however, and disrupts the peace he has provided (Holden feels sleepy for the first time) by awakening the boy with tentative homosexual advances. Certainly Holden is victimized ("I was shaking like a madman. . . . I think I was more depressed than I ever was in my life"), but the encounter may torment him most for its parallels to his own unconscious designs on a child. Now one begins to see the significance of Holden's unfounded suspicions about Jane Gallagher's stepfather and his murderous rage at the "perverty bum" who wrote the obscenity on Phoebe's school wall—inordinate reactions pointing to fears about himself.

At this point Holden's neurosis verges on madness. Each time he crosses a street, he imagines he will "disappear" and "never get to the other side of the street." I do not take this so much as a symbolic manifestation of "identity crisis" and of his fear that he "may never reach maturity"—although both are implicit—but rather as a literal, psychologically valid description of the boy's breakdown. He retreats into wild fantasies of running away forever, living in a cabin near, but not in, the woods ("I'd want it to be sunny as hell all the time"), and feigning deaf-muteness, all to escape the confusion about to engulf him. Phoebe betrays these plans—the first ironic level of the Benedict Arnold motif—by joining in his escape. When she appears, bag in hand and the hunting cap on her head, Holden reacts wildly:

> "I'm going with you. Can I? Okay?"
> "What?" I said. I almost fell over when she said that. I swear to God I did. I got sort of dizzy and I thought I was going to pass out or something again.
>
> . . . .
>
> I thought I was going to pass out cold. I mean I didn't tell her to shut up and all, but I thought I was going to pass out again.
>
> . . . .
>
> I was almost all set to hit her. I thought I was going to smack her for a second. I really did. . . .
> "I thought you were supposed to be Benedict Arnold in the play and all," I said. I said it very nasty. "Wuddaya want to do? Not be in the play, for God's sake?" That made her cry even harder. I was glad. All of a sudden I wanted her to cry until her eyes practically dropped out. I almost hated her. I think I

hated her most because she wouldn't be in that play any more
if she went away with me.

These near-hysterical responses can be understood, it seems to me, only in
the context that Phoebe is the very thing he is fleeing. He somehow realizes
that she *must* be his "Benedict Arnold."

Holden's fury at Phoebe having set the climax in motion, Salinger now
employs a delicate spatial strategy. Phoebe returns the hat, turns her back on
Holden, announces that she has no intention of running away with him, and
runs "right the hell across the street, without even looking to see if any cars
were coming." Positioning here signifies the end of their relation as possible
lovers, but love remains. Holden does not go after her, knowing she'll follow
him "on the *other* goddam side of the street. She wouldn't look over at me at
all, but I could tell she was probably watching me out of the corner of her
crazy eye to see where I was going and all. Anyway, we kept walking that way
all the way to the zoo." They are still apart as they watch the sea lions being
fed, Holden standing "right behind her."

> I didn't put my hands on her shoulders again or anything
> because if I had she *really* would've beat it on me. Kids are
> funny. You have to watch what you're doing.
>
> She wouldn't walk right next to me when we left the sea
> lions, but she didn't walk too far away. She sort of walked on
> one side of the sidewalk and I walked on the other side.
> . . . .
> Old Phoebe still wouldn't talk to me or anything, but she was
> sort of walking next to me now. I took a hold of the belt at the
> back of her coat, just for the hell of it, but she wouldn't let me.
> She said, "Keep your hands to yourself, if you don't mind."

Holden promises not to run away and they rejoin as brother and sister
in the presence of the carrousel—miraculously open in winter. Phoebe wants
to ride and Holden finds a mature, new perspective:

> All the kids were trying to grab for the gold ring, and so was
> old Phoebe, and I was sort of afraid she'd fall off the goddam
> horse, but I didn't say anything or do anything. The thing with
> kids is, if they want to grab for the gold ring, you have to let
> them do it, and not say anything. If they fall off, they fall off,
> but it's bad if you say anything to them.

The substitution of a gold ring for the traditional brass one may point to Phoebe's future as a woman. In any event, Holden has renounced his designs on Phoebe and thus abrogated his messianic role. Another Salinger story has young de Daumier-Smith relinquish his sexual designs on a nun with the announcement, "I am giving Sister Irma her freedom to follow her destiny. Everyone is a nun." One need not search for literary sources to recognize that the carrousel finally represents everyone's sacred, inviolable human destiny.

III

Readers now dubious about this paper's clinical approach ("aesthetic pathology," Salinger has called it) may wonder why I have thus far neglected to make a masculine symbol of Holden's long-peaked hunting cap—which he purchased, one recalls, after losing the fencing team's foils in a subway. This rather mechanical symbol does partake of the boy's masculinity or sexuality. But more than that, it becomes the most reliable symbolic designation of Holden's psychic condition through the novel. Ackley points out that it is a deer hunter's hat while Holden maintains that "This is a people shooting hat. . . . I shoot people in this hat." When one remembers that hunters wear red hats to keep from being shot and that Holden usually wears his backwards in the manner of a baseball catcher, the symbol embraces Holden's aggressive and withdrawing tendencies as well as the outlandish daydreams of becoming the messiah in the rye.

Holden's masculinity is plainly involved in such instances as when he has to retrieve the hat from under a bed after the fight with Stradlater and when it is entrusted to Phoebe's bed, but the symbol becomes more encompassing when she "restores" the hat in the climactic carrousel scene.

> Then all of a sudden she gave me a kiss. Then she held her hand out and said, "It's raining. It's starting to rain."
> "I know."
> Then what she did—it damn near killed me—she reached in my coat pocket and took out my red hunting hat and put it on my head.
> . . . .
> My hunting hat really gave me quite a lot of protection, in a way, but I got soaked anyway. I didn't care, though. I felt so damn happy all of a sudden, the way old Phoebe kept going around and around. I was damn near bawling, I felt so damn happy, if you want to know the truth. I don't know why. It was just that she looked so damn *nice*, the way she kept going

around and around, in her blue coat and all. God, I wish you
could have been there.

At its deepest level, the hat symbolizes something like Holden's basic
human resources—his birthright, that lucky caul of protective courage,
humor, compassion, honesty, and love—all of which are the real subject
matter of the novel.

As the symbolic hat gives Holden "quite a lot of protection, in a way"
and he gets "soaked anyway," those human resources do not prevent
emotional collapse. In the epilogue we learn that Holden went West—"after
I went home, and . . . got sick and all"—not for the traditional opportunity
there but for psychotherapy. This would be a bleak ending were it not for the
fact that Holden has authored this structured narrative, just as Antolini
predicted he might:

> "you'll find that you're not the first person who was ever
> confused and frightened and even sickened by human behavior.
> You're by no means alone on that score, you'll be excited and
> *stimulated* to know. Many, many men have been just as troubled
> morally and spiritually as you are right now. Happily, some of
> them kept records of their troubles. You'll learn from them—if
> you want to. Just as someday, if you have something to offer,
> someone will learn something from you. It's a beautiful
> reciprocal arrangement. And it isn't education. It's history. It's
> poetry."

The richness of spirit in this novel, especially of the vision, the compassion,
and the humor of the narrator reveal a psyche far healthier than that of the
boy who endured the events of the narrative. Through the telling of his
story, Holden has given shape to, and thus achieved control of, his troubled
past.

KERRY McSWEENEY

Salinger Revisited

For anyone who was a literate North-American adolescent during the 1950s, it is probably difficult, even after fifteen or twenty years, to go beyond a personal estimate and/or historical estimate of the fiction of J. D. Salinger and attempt a 'real' estimate. The task will be especially difficult for those who were in those days uncritical enthusiasts of *Nine Stories, The Catcher in the Rye* and the Glass stories; for a retrospective distaste and embarrassment over one's youthful intensities, idealisings and over-simplifications may well make for a prejudiced reading.

The possibility of overreaction on my part may be indicated by a catalogue of the Salingeresque items—tokens of sensitivity, emblems of non-aggression, touchstones of selflessness—that fell out of my copy of *Catcher* when I recently opened it for the first time in a decade and a half: *(a)* a transcript of a poem by the then Brother Antonius, which begins

> Annul in me my manhood, Lord, and make
> Me woman-sexed and weak,
> If by that total transformation
> I might know Thee more;

(b) another of a Bob Dylan song, which begins with

From *Critical Quarterly* 20, no. 1 (Spring 1978). © 1978 Manchester University Press.

I ain't looking to compete with you, beat or cheat or
    mistreat you,
Simplify you, classify you, deny, defy, or crucify you,
All I really want to do is, baby, be friends with you;

(c) a *Peanuts* cartoon, in which Linus, holding as ever his security blanket,
declares to Charlie Brown that 'No problem is so big or so complicated that
it can't be run away from'; and *(d)* a *New Yorker* cartoon of two men in dinner
jackets, holding highball glasses and looking at a wall on which are mounted
heads of a number of ferocious looking animals—except for the centrepiece:
the enormous head of a benign, quietly smiling lion, whose post-prandial
countenance echoes those of the men, one of whom is explaining that 'I was
removing a thorn from its paw when I suddenly thought: "What a
magnificent head".'

Still, one aspires to objectivity and disinterest, and there is little doubt
that now is a good time for a retrospective assessment of Salinger. For one
thing, Warren French may well be more than self-serving when he says in
the preface to the newly revised edition of his *J. D. Salinger* that 'former
readers, alienated from Salinger during the activist 1960s, are now returning
to his books with renewed interest and are commending them to their
children and their students'. For another, the Salinger canon seems
essentially complete. His last published work, the unreadable 'Hapworth 16,
1924', appeared in the *New Yorker* twelve years ago. This 'story' consisted of
an interminable letter sent from summer camp by the then *seven*-year-old
prodigy, poet, and saint, Seymour Glass. What can you say about a kid who
describes his meals thus: 'While the food itself is not atrocious, it is cooked
without a morsel of affection or inspiration, each string bean or simple carrot
arriving on the camper's plate quite stripped of its tiny vegetal soul'?
'Hapworth 16, 1924' had given the impression that Salinger had become
self-indulgent in his writing, and was withdrawing into a self-referential
fanstasy world. This seemed confirmed by the disheartening statement the
author made in 1974 when he broke a public silence of more than twenty
years to complain in a telephone interview with the *New York Times* about the
publication of an unauthorised collection of his apprentice work: 'There is a
marvellous peace in not publishing. It's peaceful. Still. Publishing is a terrible
invasion of my privacy. I like to write. I love to write. But I write just for
myself and my own pleasure.'

The first of his works that Salinger regarded as post-apprentice were
among those included in his 1954 collection, *Nine Stories*. All these stories are
set in the only world Salinger knows: that of upper middle class New York
City. They contain an abundance of acute social notation: Salinger is
particularly good at using the details of speech, dress and decor to register

the nuances of social stratification and character type. The world of the stories is mimed by Salinger's characteristic prose: The mannered *New Yorker* style of coy hyperbole and sophisticated overstatement, the knowing tone, and the self-conscious, mandarin poise tempered by measured colloquialisms.

While Salinger clearly finds much that is wrong with the world he describes, unlike Flaubert or Joyce he does not reveal his disapproval through his style, which in fact tends to exemplify the values of that world. This important point was made by Frank Kermode in 1962: 'the really queer thing about this writer is that he carefully writes for an audience [a culture-acquisitive audience] he deplores.' To put the matter differently: while there is in *Nine Stories*, as in the rest of Salinger, much excellent social observation, albeit of a very narrow part of the social spectrum, there is very little social vision because Salinger has no outside point of view to bring to bear on a world to which he can imagine no positive, post-puberty alternative and of which, *faute de mieux*, he remains a part. Philip Roth overstated the case in 1962, but one understands his exasperation: 'the problem of how to live *in* this world is by no means answered . . . The only advice we seem to get from Salinger is to be charming on the way to the loony bin.'

The dominant subject of *Nine Stories* is the opposition of the few (the sensitive, delicate and discerning, usually children or disturbed young men) and the many (the crass, insensitive and phony). The upshot of this opposition can be destructive: the first and last stories, 'A perfect day for bananafish' and 'Teddy', end abruptly with the suicide of the representative of the few. But when two sensitive, non-aggressive souls can make contact, a more optimistic, even sentimental, conclusion becomes possible, as in 'De Daumier-Smith's blue period' and 'For Esmé—with love and squalor', for the latter of which, despite the narrator's Dostoyevskian rumblings, this quotation from *Silas Marner* would have made a perfect epigraph: 'In old days there were angels who came and took men by the hand and led them away from the city of destruction. We see no white-winged angels now. But yet men are led away from threatening destruction: a hand is put into theirs, which leads them gently towards a calm and bright land, so that they look no more backward; and the hand may be a little child's.'

Of course, some of the *Nine Stories* are better than others. One of the finest, 'Uncle Wiggily in Connecticut', has at its centre the quintessential Salinger theme of the true life which is absent. In *Zooey*, Franny Glass, on the brink of a breakdown, will say that the one person she wants to talk to is her dead brother Seymour; in *Catcher*, Holden Caulfield, when challenged to name just one person whom he really likes, will choose his dead brother Allie. In 'Uncle Wiggily' two old friends, Mary Jane and Eloise, get together in the latter's suburban home for an afternoon of reminiscence, complaint and too much drink. As their conversation becomes intimate, Eloise begins to speak of the young man, a brother of Seymour Glass, who was different (the story's title alludes to one of his fey witticisms); who was in fact everything that her husband is not; whom she loved; and who was killed in an absurd accident during the war. The loss is nicely counterpointed by the relationship of Eloise's young daughter to her imaginary friend, Jimmy Jimmereeno. When Jimmy is run over, his place in the daughter's bed is taken by Mickey Mickeranno. But Eloise cannot make contact with her daughter—she even insists on making her sleep in the middle of the bed as a way of negating Mickey's existence—and for her there is nothing to fill the absence of Walt Glass except her maudlin insistence at the end of the story that she used to be a nice girl.

On the other hand, 'De Daumier-Smith's blue period', which has a similar theme, is a weak story. Its narrator is a sensitive young man stuck in a cheesy art correspondence school in Montreal, who becomes unilaterally involved through the mail with a nun in Toronto whose work shows promise but whose superiors unexpectedly require her to withdraw from the school. The nun, a variant of the Salingeresque child figure, is of course an embodiment of the absent true life for which the narrator yearns. The story's events take place when the narrator is nineteen; he is thirty-two when he recounts them (the same age, incidentally, as Salinger when he wrote the story, just as the narrator's initials are identical with the author's). But the older narrator is indistinguishable from his younger self; there is no distancing, no perspective, no way of placing or grounding, the epiphany with which the story concludes. Gazing into the window of an orthopedic appliances shop, De Daumier-Smith suddenly has 'an extraordinary experience', a moment of vision which leaves 'twice blessed' the objects in the window and leads to the assertion that he can give up Sister Irma because 'Everybody is a nun. (*Tout le monde est une nonne*).' This climactic moment, a harbinger of the notorious ending of *Zooey*, where it is asserted that the Fat Lady is Christ, seems to me quite hollow and unearned, and, like the narrator, immature and callow. 'Twice blessed' is an empty poeticism borrowed (probably unconsciously) from Portia's speech in *The Merchant of Venice*. And 'Everybody is a nun' recalls the '*Tout est grâce*' at the end of Bernanos' great novel, *Journal d'un curé de campagne*, in a way that devastatingly points up the thinness, staginess, and merely notional quality of Salinger's scene.

One generalisation that could be made about these two stories involves the old chestnut about the relative difficulty in creating convincing fictional representations of unfallen as opposed to fallen, transcendent to quotidian, gain to loss, saint to sinner, selflessness to egotism. Salinger seems to be aware of this problem in that 'De Daumier-Smith's blue period' contains a degree of narrative self-consciousness (absent in 'Uncle Wiggily') which suggests uneasiness in the face of a difficult creative problem. For the same reason, narrative self-consciousness becomes more and more prominent in the four Glass family stories which began to appear in *The New Yorker* the year after the publication of *Nine Stories.*

One thing that can be said about all of the *Nine Stories* is that they are professional pieces of work, textbook examples of the short-story form. By the same token, despite a good deal of ingenuity, they are limited by the form's conventional boundaries. One senses Salinger's dissatisfaction with this, and sees him beginning to push beyond the boundaries in 'Franny.' As in the *Nine Stories,* the subject of this long short story is the opposition of the phony and the seeker after authenticity. Again, it is the phony—the splendid figure of Lane Coutell—that is better done. The presentation of Franny, an equally recognizable social type (a female Ivy Leaguer), is more fuzzy and uncertain. Particularly telling is the fact that Salinger can only convey a sense of Franny's spiritual yearnings by having her summarize the contents of a Russian religious work, cry a lot, and continually mumble the Jesus prayer.

In 'Raise high the roof beam, carpenters', a novella-length short story (it is not a short novella), the same contrast is in some ways better handled. The members of the wedding-party diaspora who eventually gather in Buddy and Seymour Glass's apartment are the rather too exhaustively detailed equivalent of the Lane Coutell world. The contrasting figure is again a Glass sibling, this time Seymour, like Franny a quasi-mystic, a seeker after higher truth who is half drawn towards, half put off by sexual and emotional involvement (for Franny, Lane; for Seymour, Muriel).

It is in the contrast between Seymour and Franny that the superiority of 'Raise high the roof-beam, carpenters' lies. Seymour is a much stronger and more convincing representation of spirituality. The principal reason for this is that he never appears in the story. He is the true life whose absence is mediated by his loving brother Buddy, the narrator. Because Salinger does not present Seymour directly he can become an acceptable, almost palpable representative of the higher life. Even his metaphorical stigmata—'I have scars on my hands from touching certain people' (from a diary Buddy has found)—which seems particularly annoying to certain critics, seems to me a striking evocation of what George Eliot called 'a keen vision and feeling of all ordinary human life', which if we had them would be 'like hearing the grass grow and the squirrel's heart beat' and cause us to 'die of that roar which lies on the other side of silence'.

The two other Glass stories, 'Zooey' and 'Seymour: an introduction', are both disappointing pieces of work, much shrunken from the dimensions they had for me in the late 1950s. Both, particularly the latter, represent an interesting technical development in Salinger's art, for in them he has broken away completely from the conventional short-story form. This has been mainly achieved through the increased self-consciousness of the author/narrator and his active involvement in the story he is trying to tell. As Philip Roth was perhaps the first to recognise, in these stories Salinger was concerned 'to place the figure of the writer directly in the reader's line of vision'. (More recently, in a piece in the 13 June 1975 *TLS*, David Lodge has suggestively discussed the 'elaborate game with his audience and with the conventions of his art' that the later Salinger is playing). For example, in 'Seymour: an introduction' the subject of the story is as much the creative difficulties of Buddy Glass in presenting to the reader his saintly brother ('the one person who was always much, much too large to fit on ordinary typewriter paper') as it is Seymour himself. The spiritual theme (Seymour) and the epistemological/aesthetic theme (the apprehension and presentation of Seymour) become indistinguishable and are simultaneously held in the matrix of the writer-reader relationship.

It is from this technical point of view that 'Zooey' and 'Seymour: an introduction' are most interesting. But this is not enough to save either story from its content. There is too much in the 44,000 words of 'Zooey' that is self-indulgent and inert; and the presentation and resolution of the religious problem is pitched in so shrill a key that one eventually comes to see that Salinger has taken Franny's rather run-of-the-mill collegiate identity crisis and tried to do much-too-much with it. And both the closing affirmation at the end of the 27,000 words of 'Seymour: an introduction' ('all we do our whole lives is go from one little piece of Holy Ground to the next') and its climactic epiphany (the apparition of Seymour at 'the magic hour of the day' during a marble shooting game and his admonishing Buddy not to aim), though the latter once seemed to me the most incandescent moment in Salinger's canon, now seem too meagre and too much like cut-rate Zen to justify the expenditure of time and energy necessary to get to the end of the story.

The only work of Salinger's that has not shrunk with the passage of time is *The Catcher in the Rye*. The macro-subject of Salinger's only novel is that of all his fiction; as Carol and Richard Ohmann say in their provocative 'case study of capitalist criticism' of *Catcher* in the autumn 1976 *Critical Inquiry*, the novel is 'among other things a serious critical mimesis of bourgeois life in the Eastern United States ca. 1950'. The micro-subject is a crisis-point in the adolescence of a sensitive and perceptive youth: Holden Caulfield is sixteen when the events in the novel take place; seventeen when he narrates them. The social notation is superb: the expensive prep school with its Ackleys and Stradlaters; the lobby of the Biltmore (the *in* place for dates to meet); the Greenwich Village bar and the equally tony Wicker Bar uptown; the crowd in the theatre lobby at intermission; Mr. and Mrs. Antolini; the sad 'girls' from Seattle who are in the big city to have a good time; and so on.

Similarly, the macro-theme of *Catcher* is that of the rest of Salinger; the almost Dickensian dichotomy between the lower world of the many and the innocent, constantly threatened world of the few: the dead Allie, who used to write poems all over his baseball mitt, and Jane Gallagher, who when playing checkers always kept her kings in the back row (both activities recall Seymour's admonition not to aim when shooting marbles); the two nuns who 'went around collecting dough in those beat-up old straw baskets'; and Phoebe, the wise child, for love of whom her exhausted brother is moved to tears on the novel's last page.

What is different in *Catcher*, and what must be considered the key to its success, is its method. Holden's first person narration *ipso facto* removes from the novel any trace of *New Yorker* preciosities. Everything is seen from Holden's point of view and reported in his pungent vernacular. The voice and the perceptions are wholly convincing and of sustained freshness. Indeed, the only comparatively flat scenes—on the train with Morrow's mother, in the restaurant with the nuns—are the two places in the novel where one feels that there is something derivative about Holden's characterisation and narration, that he is drawn more from *Huckleberry Finn* than from life.

Holden's adolescent perspective, halfway between the childhood and adult worlds, fully a part of neither yet acutely sensitive to and observant of both, provides the perfect point of focus for *Catcher*. Holden is in a privileged though precarious position. A two- or three-year difference in his age, in either direction, would have made for an entirely different book. In his own image, to which the novel's title calls attention, Holden is 'on the edge of some crazy cliff', with little kids playing in a field of rye on one side of him, an abyss on the other. Like that of Nick Carraway, Fitzgerald's narrator in *The Great Gatsby*, Holden's bifocal vision allows him simultaneously to register both the phoniness and meretriciousness of the fallen world and the sense of wonder and tenderness, and the supernal *frissons*, of the innocent world. And since they are so well grounded (and thereby authenticated) in a particular person at a particular time of life, Holden's longings, needs and intimations of mystery never become sentimental or merely notional. Indeed they are the most resonant images in all of Salinger of the longing for the absent true life, as in Holden's haunting question of where the Central Park ducks go in the winter, his love for the dead brother, and for the live sister whom he wishes could, like things in the museum, always stay the way she now is and never have to grow up.

Near the end of *Catcher* Holden reflects that there is no place where one is free from somebody sneaking up and writing 'Fuck you' right under your nose. Holden's erasures of this phrase recall the last page of *The Great Gatsby* when Nick Carraway deletes an obscene word from Gatsby's steps before going down to the water's edge to begin his great meditation on the capacity for wonder and the longing for absent true life, which draws one ceaselessly back into the past. There are more similarities between Fitzgerald's and Salinger's novels (and between the two authors) than might at first meet the eye, and a brief concluding comparison of the two may be of help in making a stab at gauging the 'real' status of *Catcher*.

Both novels turn on the contrast of a fallen world of aggression, selfishness and phoniness and a tenuous higher world of (to use Fitzgerald's phrase) 'heightened sensitivity to the promises of life'. Both writers have been charged with having no real social vision to complement their acute social notation: what the Ohmanns say of Holden Caulfield may, *mutatis mutandis*, be said of his creator: 'for all his perceptiveness . . . he is an adolescent with limited understanding of what he perceives'. And Fitzgerald has of course been described as having been taken in by what he could see through. I believe that this remark is manifestly unfair to Fitzgerald at his best, and that there is much to ponder in his (admittedly oddly phrased) notebook comment that D. H. Lawrence was 'Essential[ly] pre-Marxian. Just as I am essentially Marxian.' There is real social insight in *Gatsby*, which offers a complex anatomy and moral evaluation of the world it describes. Because its bifocal vision is that of a discriminating adult, not that of an engagingly screwed-up teenager, the novel is able to offer a richer and more complex exploration both of the lower world and the higher world of threatened innocence and longing.

For these reasons, among others, *Gatsby* seems to me an appreciably greater novel than *Catcher*. But the difference is perhaps one of degree rather than of kind, and if one accepts John Berryman's definition of a masterpiece (found in his excellent essay on *Gatsby* in *The Freedom of the Poet*)—

> a work of the literary imagination which is consistent, engaging, and dramatic, in exceptional degrees; which exhibits largely mastered a human subject of the first importance; and which seems in retrospect to illuminate the whole physical and spiritual situation of which it was, by the strange parturition of art, an accidental product. One easy test will be the rapidity with which, in the imagination of a good judge, other works of

the period and kind will faint away under any suggested comparison with it.

—one may go on to say that both *The Great Gatsby* and *The Catcher in the Rye* belong on permanent display in the gallery of classic American fiction.

EDWIN HAVILAND MILLER

In Memoriam: Allie Caulfield in The Catcher in the Rye

Although J. D. Salinger's *Catcher in the Rye* deserves the affection and accolades it has received since its publication in 1951, whether it has been praised for the right reasons is debatable. Most critics have tended to accept Holden's evaluation of the world as phony, when in fact his attitudes are symptomatic of a serious psychological problem. Thus instead of treating the novel as a commentary by an innocent young man rebelling against an insensitive world or as a study of a youth's moral growth, I propose to read *Catcher in the Rye* as the chronicle of a four-year period in the life of an adolescent whose rebelliousness is his only means of dealing with his inability to come to terms with the death of his brother. Holden Caulfield has to wrestle not only with the usual difficult adjustments of the adolescent years, in sexual, familial and peer relationships; he has also to bury Allie before he can make the transition into adulthood.

Life stopped for Holden on July 18, 1946, the day his brother died of leukemia. Holden was then thirteen, and four years later—the time of the narrative—he is emotionally still at the same age, although he has matured into a gangly six-foot adolescent. "I was sixteen then," he observes concerning his expulsion from Pencey Prep at Christmas time in 1949, "and I'm seventeen now, and sometimes I act like I'm about thirteen."

On several occasions Holden comments that his mother has never

From *Mosaic* 15, no. 1 (Winter 1982). © 1982 *Mosaic*.

gotten over Allie's death, which may or may not be an accurate appraisal of Mrs. Caulfield, since the first-person narrative makes it difficult to judge. What we can deduce, though, is that it is an accurate appraisal of Holden's inability to accept loss, and that in his eyes his mother is so preoccupied with Allie that she continues to neglect Holden, as presumably she did when Allie was dying.

The night after Allie's death Holden slept in the garage and broke "all the goddam windows with my fist, just for the hell of it. I even tried to break all the windows on the station wagon we had that summer, but my hand was already broken and everything by the time, and I couldn't do it. It was a very stupid thing to do, I'll admit, but I hardly didn't even know I was doing it, and you didn't know Allie." The act may have been "stupid"—which is one of his pet words to denigrate himself as well as others—but it also reflects his uncontrollable anger, at himself for wishing Allie dead and at his brother for leaving him alone and burdened with feelings of guilt. Similarly, the attack on the station wagon may be seen as his way of getting even with a father who was powerless either to save Allie or to understand Holden. Because he was hospitalized, he was unable to attend the funeral, to witness the completion of the life process, but by injuring himself he received the attention and sympathy which were denied him during Allie's illness. His actions here as elsewhere are inconsistent and ambivalent, but always comprehensible in terms of his reaction to the loss of Allie.

So too is Holden's vocabulary an index to his disturbed emotional state—for all that it might seem to reflect the influence of the movies or his attempts to imitate the diction of his older brother, D. B. At least fifty times, something or somebody *depresses* him—an emotion which he frequently equates with a sense of isolation: "It makes you feel so lonesome and depressed." Although the reiteration of the word reveals the true nature of his state, no one in the novel recognizes the signal, perceiving the boy as a kind of adolescent clown rather than as a seriously troubled youth. As his depression deepens to the point of nervous breakdown, furthermore, Holden—who at some level of awareness realizes that he is falling apart— seeks to obscure the recognition by referring to everything as "crazy" and by facetiously likening himself to a "madman."

"Crap," another word he uses repeatedly, is similarly self-reflexive. Although it is his ultimate term of reductionism for describing the world, like "crazy" it serves to identify another of his projections. He feels dirty and worthless, and so makes the world a reflection of his self-image. Similarly, if he continually asserts, almost screams, that the phony world makes him want to "puke," it is because Holden's world itself has turned to vomit. In his troubled, almost suicidal state he can incorporate nothing, and, worse, he believes there is nothing for him to incorporate. In turn, the significance of his repeated use of variations on the phrase "that killed me" becomes almost self-evident: reflecting his obsession with death, it tells the unsuspecting world that he wishes himself dead, punished and then reunited with Allie.

Although his consistently negative and hostile language thus reflects Holden's despair and is his way of informing the world of his plight, if no one listens it is primarily his own fault. For with the usual fumbling of the hurt he has chosen a means which serves his purposes poorly. While his language may serve to satisfy his need to act out his anger, at the same time it serves to isolate and to punish him further. If in his hostile phrases he is calling for help, he makes certain that he does not receive it. Ashamed of his need—a sixteen-year old crying for emotional support—and unable to accept kindness since in his guilt he feels he does not deserve it, Holden is locked into his grief and locked out of family and society.

In this respect, the first paragraph of *Catcher in the Rye* is one of the most deceptively revealing possible. Although Holden, the would-be sophisticate, relegates his familial background to "David Copperfield kind of crap," he talks about little else except his "lousy childhood." Arguing that he will not divulge family secrets so as not to cause pain, and pretending to respect the feelings of his parents, he verbally mutilates them, and in an ugly way; but if he is to suffer, so must they. He retaliates in kind, not in kindness. Yet the aggressive, assertive tone masks a pitiful, agonized call for emotional support and love.

Equally revealing of Holden's problem is his observation, as he stands alone on a hill that cold December, his last day at Pencey Prep, looking down at the football field where his classmates are participating collectively in one of the rites of adolescence: "it was cold as a witch's teat, especially on top of that stupid hill." What he wants is the good mother's breast. And why he needs this maternal comfort so much is implicitly suggested when he descends the hill to say good-by to his history teacher, who cannot understand why in answering a question about Egyptian history on an examination Holden should have begun and ended with a description of the preservation of mummies. The teacher cannot know that Holden has no interest in the Egyptians, only in what happened to Allie, and that he cannot focus on ancient history until he has come to terms with his own past. Nor can he know that Holden has misinterpreted as rejection his father's concern for his future, that the boy wants to be at home, and that to accomplish his goal he has failed in four different schools.

But lest one think that this insensitivity is a fault of the older generation, Salinger next portrays the response of one of Holden's peers to the first of a number of roles he will play in his desperate attempt to disguise his obsession with Allie's death, on the one hand, and his need for parental comfort, on the other. Thus when Holden pulls his red hunting cap over his eyes and says histrionically, "I think I'm going blind. . . . Mother darling, everything's getting so *dark* in here. . . . Mother darling, give me your hand," the response of his classmate is: "You're nuts. . . . For Chrisake, grow up." Ackley cannot know that Holden assumes Allie's red hair when he puts on the red cap, that the simulated blindness is descriptive of Holden's state, or that he uses the script as a (futile) means of asking for the maternal hand that he believes has been denied to him.

If Ackley does not appreciate the extent to which the death of Holden's red-haired brother informs his posturing, even less is his room-mate Stradlater aware of the chain of associations that he sets off when he asks Holden to write a composition for him. Unable to write about a "room or a house" Holden writes about Allie's baseball mitt—an object which is a complex version of a child's security blanket, a sacred relic of the living dead, at the same time that it reminds Holden of betrayal. And thus as he writes about the mitt, we learn directly for the first time of Allie's death and of Holden's self-punishing rage.

By coincidence, Stradlater has a date that evening with Jane Gallagher, the girl to whom Holden had shown the glove in a combined attempt to sympathize with her for her unhappy childhood and to solicit her sympathy for himself. Worried that Stradlater will make "time" with an attractive girl with whom Holden plays checkers—the only kind of play of which the self-styled sex maniac is capable—Holden presses to know what has happened on the date. And when Stradlater implies that he got what he wanted, Holden lashes out with the hand he injured on the day of Allie's death. Subsequently pinned to the floor until he promises to stop his ridiculing insults, as soon as he is released, Holden shouts, "You're a dirty stupid sonuvabitch of a moron," and then he receives the blow that subconsciously he wants. "You asked for it, God damn it," Stradlater says, and he is right for reasons he does not understand.

And so on his last day at Pencey Prep Holden makes a clean sweep of it: he writes off the school, his chums, and even Jane. There is no Tom Sawyer to rescue him when he eventually quotes Huck Finn: "I felt so lonesome, all of a sudden. I almost wished I was dead." Suddenly Holden decides to leave late that evening even though his family is not expecting him until the following Wednesday. His Mark Cross luggage packed, he is "sort of crying. I don't know why. I put my hunting hat on, and turned the peak around to the back, the way I liked it, and then I yelled at the top of my goddam voice, '*Sleep tight, ya morons!*'" Thus, in his usual hostile fashion Holden makes sure that he will be rejected. Protected only by the red hat, which he now wears like a baseball catcher as he evokes Allie's favorite sport, he stumbles down the stairs and "damn near broke my crazy neck."

On the train to New York he strikes up a conversation with a Mrs. Morrow, who turns out to be the mother of one of his former classmates. He lies through his teeth praising her son who is "about as sensitive as a goddam toilet seat." But "Mothers are all slightly insane. The thing is, though, I liked old Morrow's mother," who happens to be proud of her moronic son. When she wonders whether Holden is leaving school before the beginning of vacation "because of illness in the family," he casually informs her, "I have this tiny little tumor on the brain." The fib achieves the expected result, Mrs. Morrow's genuine sympathy for an ill "son."

Though Holden plans to spend the next few days in a hotel, he is "so damn absent-minded" that he gives the cab driver his home address. After he realizes his "mistake," they drive through Central Park, and Holden asks the driver whether he knows what happens to the ducks in the pond during the winter. The "madman" replies angrily, "What're ya tryna do, bud? . . . Kid me?" Worried that he has antagonized the man, Holden invites him for a drink. When the driver refuses, Holden, "depressed," retaliates against "father": "He was one of those bald guys that comb all their hair over from the side to cover up the baldness."

In the hotel he is bored but "feeling pretty horny," as a sixteen-year-old is supposed to feel, and he calls up a whore but lets her put him off ("I *really* fouled that up.") Then he thinks of telephoning his sister Phoebe, who "has this sort of red hair, a little bit like Allie's was," but he is afraid his mother will answer. He goes to the bar in the hotel and dances with some older women from Seattle who are in New York to see the celebrities, not to provide Holden with entertainment or solace. He punishes them for neglecting him when he fibs that Gary Cooper has just left the room. On the way to a bar frequented by his older brother D.B., who is now, according to Holden, prostituting himself in Hollywood, he asks a cabby named Horwitz about the ducks in the lagoon in Central Park. Horwitz gets "sore" and counters in a typical New York taxi discussion that "The *fish* don't go no place." Desperate for companionship, Holden invites Horwitz for a drink. The driver refuses and has the last word: "If you was a fish, Mother Nature'd take care of *you*, wouldn't she? Right? You don't think them fish just *die*, when it gets to be winter, do ya?" Holden does not comment, but Horwitz unwittingly summarizes the boy's dilemma.

Later, in D.B.'s nightclub Holden glosses over his loneliness by observing the behavior of the phonies in the club, and then rejects the invitation of one of D.B.'s girl friends as others have rejected him. When Holden returns to his hotel, an elevator operator named Maurice sets him up with a call girl, but when "Sunny" arrives, he is "more depressed than sexy," and asks her to stay and talk. He pays her $5.00 and then "depressed" begins "talking, sort of out loud, to Allie."

Maurice returns with Sunny and demands another $5.00 for services not rendered. Holden tries to defend his rights but begins to cry. Sunny wants to leave quietly after she takes money from Holden's wallet, but Maurice "snapped his finger very hard on my pajamas. I won't tell you *where* he snapped it, but it hurt like hell." (The sudden self-protective chastity is an amusing and effective detail.) When Holden calls Maurice "a stupid chiseling moron" for the second time that evening he is smacked, with a "terrific punch" in his stomach. Hardly able to breathe, fearing he is drowning, he stumbles toward the bathroom. "Crazy," he acts out a scenario: with a bullet in his gut, he goes down the stairs and puts six shots into Maurice's "fat hairy belly," and then throws the gun down the elevator shaft. He calls up Jane, who comes over and bandages his wound: "I pictured her holding a cigarette for me to smoke while I was bleeding and all." Finally he goes to sleep: "What I really felt like, though, was commiting suicide. I felt like jumping out the window. I probably would have done it, too"—except for the "stupid rubbernecks."

Holden's protestations to the contrary, the associations in this scene are only superficially from the "goddam movies." Maurice threatens Holden with castration, even though he has not had sex with Sunny, and then pummels him in the stomach. In retaliation Holden commits parricide. In his fantasy he summons Jane, who is associated with Allie through her knowledge of the baseball mitt, and has her play the role of mother.

When Holden thinks about jumping out the window, he is recalling an event which the reader does not learn about until later. A few years earlier Jimmy Castle, a classmate, was so tortured and brutalized, presumably genitally, by a bunch of students that he leaped from a window, wearing Holden's turtleneck sweater. As though Holden is not sufficiently burdened with his unresolved grief for Allie, he has had to cope with this tie to an unfortunate classmate. Sunny, the prostitute, anticipates the appearance of Phoebe, who is both the kid sister and by mythic association the sun goddess. Sunny offers Holden sex, Phoebe will offer him love. Unable to handle sex, Holden wants Sunny to be a confidante, a role which she is unable to handle. Yet she tries unsuccessfully to protect him from Maurice's aggression, which may be Holden's construction of his mother's ineffectual role in the Caulfield household.

At breakfast on the following morning he meets two nun school teachers, and begins a conversation which shortly turns to *Romeo and Juliet*. If the scene with Sunny reveals that Holden is not ready for sexual relationships—he is a "sex maniac" only in his head—his comments on the tragedy solely in terms of Romeo's culpability in Mercutio's death confirm the arrestment. He is attracted to the nuns, or mothers, who remind him of "old Ernest Morrow's mother," but they also remind him that his father was a Catholic until he "married my mother." This leads him to recall some unpleasant associations with Catholics, and when he says good-by to the nuns, "by mistake I blew some smoke in their faces. I didn't mean to, but I did it." In atonement for his unkindness Holden makes a symbolic apology to the nuns when he imagines them standing in front of a department store raising money for charity. He tries to "picture my mother or somebody, or my aunt, or Sally Hayes's crazy mother, standing outside some department store and collecting dough for poor people in a beat-up old straw hat. It was hard to picture." Since his "picture" of his mother is too harsh, and anxiety-producing, he guiltily corrects it: "Not so much my mother, but those other two."

Walking along the street, he sees a family coming from church—"a father, a mother, and a little kid about six years old." Holden "sees" the family, but only in terms of his own situation. Without evidence he initially assumes that the parents are neglecting the boy who walks along the curb singing to himself, "If a body catch a body coming through the rye"—or so Holden imagines. For it is doubtful that the six-year-old, if he knows the poem in the first place, duplicates Holden's misreading of the famous lines. What Holden "hears" anticipates the grandiose fantasy he will later relate to Phoebe in which he catches and saves children. For a moment he is charmed with his fantasy of a self-contained kid whose parents are at hand to protect him: "It made me feel not so depressed any more."

In the afternoon Holden escorts Sally Hayes to a Broadway show and goes ice skating at Rockefeller Center. Then they sit down for a chat—about Holden. He pours out his anger at the phony world, and when Sally tries to be sensible, he almost screams at her. "I don't get hardly anything out of anything. I'm in bad shape. I'm in *lousy* shape." Sally can hardly be expected to understand how empty he feels, or know how to respond to his cry for sympathy. Then he proposes what he knows she cannot agree to, that they run off together to New England. When she objects to the scheme, he verbally assaults her but not without self-pity: "she was depressing the hell out of me."

After this rejection, which in his usual fashion he makes inevitable, he tries to lift the depression by evoking earlier, happier days when the Caulfield family was intact. He goes to Radio City Music Hall, where, with the parents in another part of the theater, Allie and he had sat by themselves watching a favorite drummer. But pleasant memories of Allie cannot rescue him, and he goes to a bar to meet a former classmate named Luce. Although Holden wants Luce's companionship and assistance, he subjects him to an offensive, crude interrogation about his sex life. Twice Luce asks, repeating the question put earlier by Ackley, "When are you going to grow up?" After Holden confesses that his sex life "stinks," Luce reminds him that once before he had advised him to see an analyst. At once Holden asks for more information and comes as close as his pride permits to begging for the kind of aid which Luce of course cannot provide. When Luce gets ready to leave for his date, Holden implores, "Have just one more drink. Please. I'm lonesome as hell."

Now "*really* drunk" and wounded, because Luce like the others betrays him, he replays the scenario of "that stupid business with the bullet in my guts again. I was the only guy at the bar with a bullet in their guts. I kept putting my hand under my jacket, on my stomach and all, to keep the blood from dripping all over the place. I didn't want anybody to know I was even wounded. I was con*ceal*ing the fact that I was a wounded sonuvabitch." Even in fantasy his self-pity turns into self-disparagement: he hates himself as he screams for attention.

He decides to call up Jane Gallagher, but by "mistake"—it is almost a comedy of errors—he dials Sally Hayes and makes up for his insults. Then he goes to the men's room, dunks his head in a washbowl, and sits on a radiator to dry himself. When the pianist, "a flitty-looking guy," enters, Holden asks him to arrange a date with the singer at the club. The pianist tells him to go home.

> "You oughta go on the radio," I said. "Handsome chap like you. All those goddam golden locks. Ya need a manager?"
> "Go home, Mac, like a good guy. Go home and hit the sack."
> "No home to go to. No kidding—you need a manager?"

Holden, who needs "a manager," is crying as he goes for his coat. When the middle-aged attendant gives him his coat even though he has lost his check, he returns the kindness by asking her for a date. She laughs, but not derisively, and, intuiting the role he wants her to play, makes him put on his red hunting hat. His teeth chattering, Holden goes to Central Park to "see what the hell the ducks were doing." On the way, one "accident" following another, he drops the phonograph record he has bought for Phoebe. If, as he believes, nothing has been given to him, he cannot give even to his favorite sister and must punish her as he has been punished. When he finds the pond he nearly falls in. "Still shivering like a bastard," he imagines that he has pneumonia and dies.

In this fantasy he acts out his anger against his parents and inflicts upon them the ultimate punishment, his death. His funeral is mobbed and everybody cries: "They all came when Allie died, the whole goddam stupid bunch of them." He feels "sorry as hell for my mother and father. Especially my mother, because she still isn't over my brother Allie yet." In this reenactment of Allie's funeral he displaces his brother and enjoys exclusively the love of his mother. But not for long, since his "picture" cannot lift his guilt, dissolve his rage, or make over reality. People will not mourn him long, no longer than they mourned Allie, and life in the phony world will go on without him. Like Allie he will lie in the cemetery exposed to the elements.

To take his "mind off getting pneumonia and all," he skips "the quarters and the nickel," across the lagoon. "I don't know why I did it, but I did it." Perhaps he imitates a game Allie and he played together, but when he throws away his money, there is only one place he can go—home. Which he does, although he disguises the desire by preserving his fantasy: he goes there to see Phoebe "in case I died and all." In the foyer of the Caulfield apartment he recognizes "a funny smell that doesn't smell like any place else," and he finds Phoebe asleep in D.B.'s bed: "I felt swell for a change." Safe and protected, he begins to relax and no longer worries "whether they'd catch me home or not." What he does not say is that he would like to be caught. At first Phoebe is "very affectionate" until she guesses that he has been kicked out of Pencey Prep. Then, hurt and angry, a reaction which he cannot understand, she beats him with her fists and says over and over, "Daddy'll *kill* you!" At last Holden tellingly replies, "No, he won't. The worst he'll do, he'll give me hell again, and then he'll send me to that goddam military school. That's all he'll do."

In this climactic scene Phoebe plays a double role. About Allie's age when he died, she is the sister disappointed in the failures of her idealized brother, but she is also an underaged, undersized mother figure. Firmly but affectionately Phoebe presses Holden to explain why he has been expelled. He pours forth all his phony rationalizations, most of which begin and end with something or somebody "depressing" him. When Phoebe suggests that the fault may be his—"You don't like anything that's happening"—he is "even more depressed." She insists, now perhaps not unlike the lawyer father, that he name some things he likes. Unable to "concentrate" on her disturbing questions, Holden thinks of the two nuns and of Jimmy Castle's suicide— kind mothers and a dead son. Relentlessly but not without a concession, Phoebe asks him to tell her "one thing" he likes.

"I like Allie," I said. "And I like what I'm doing right now. Sitting here with you, and talking, and thinking about stuff, and—"

"Allie's *dead*—You always say that! If somebody's dead and everything, and in *Heaven*, then it isn't really—"

"I know he's dead! Don't you think I know that? I can still like him, though, can't I? Just because somebody's dead, you don't just stop liking them, for God's sake—especially if they were about a thousand times nicer than the people you know that're *alive* and all."

Phoebe is silent. Holden believes that "she can't think of anything to say." More perceptive than her older brother, she gives him time to recognize the significance of what he has said: that Allie is dead. Then, like the parents and the teachers, but with an affection that dilutes his anger, she tries to direct Holden to a consideration of a future which—as she tactfully does not say—must be lived without Allie. When she suggests that he may want to be a lawyer, Holden is unable to reply precisely, not merely because he is trapped in his own negations, but also because, in spite of his anger, he can only attack the father by indirection. "Lawyers are all right, I guess," he replies, with wayward antecedents, "but it does not appeal to me." He draws a picture of lawyers "saving innocent guys' lives"—which is another rescue fantasy and a disguised self-reference. When he discusses, from his hurt viewpoint, the role of the corporation lawyer, he deflects the indictment of his father through use of the second-person pronoun: "All you do is make a lot of dough and play golf and play bridge and buy cars and drink Martinis and look like a hot-shot." Ironically, Holden emulates his father's behavior, from his Mark Cross luggage to his drinking and "hot-shot" attacks on phonies.

Soon Holden confides his most heroic fantasy, undeterred when Phoebe corrects the misquotation of Burns's poem on which it is based.

> "I thought it was 'If a body catch a body,'" I said. "Anyway, I keep picturing all these little kids playing some game in this big field of rye and all. Thousands of little kids, and nobody's around—nobody big, I mean—except me. And I'm standing on the edge of some crazy cliff. What I have to do, I have to catch everybody if they start to go over the cliff—I mean if they're running and they don't look where they're going I have to come out from somewhere and *catch* them. That's all I'd do all day. I'd just be the catcher in the rye and all. I know it's crazy, but that's the only thing I'd really like to be. I know it's crazy."

This is the most complex of all the rescue fantasies. Holden has the "crazy" idea that he should have saved Allie, and that in the future he will save children abused by adults. If he is savior, he is also victim. For he himself is at "the edge of some crazy cliff" and feels himself, as he puts it later, going "down, down, down." He acts out the role he wants the adult world, particularly his father, to play: that of rescuer.

When a moment later Phoebe and Holden horse around and dance about the bedroom, the youth's delight illuminates his desire for a childhood where there are no fears, only joy and protection. The idyll ends abruptly when the parents come home, and Holden, fearing rejection, hides in a closet. Before he leaves, he borrows Phoebe's Christmas money. For the fourth time he begins to cry: "I couldn't help it. I did it so nobody could hear me, but I did it." For the first time he achieves what he has cried for from the beginning: Phoebe, now the mother, not the little sister, "put her old arm around my neck, and I put my arm around her, too, but I still couldn't stop for a long time." Before he goes, he almost tells the truth about himself as well as about the catcher-in-the-rye fantasy. "I didn't give much of a damn any more if they caught me. I really didn't. I figured if they caught me, they caught me. I almost wished they did, in a way."

Holden leaves to spend the night with a former teacher at a preparatory school, now an English professor at New York University. Antolini has been a role model, a good father, for Holden: he carried the body of Jimmy Castle to the infirmary after his suicide, and he banters in the witty style of D.B. Holden is disappointed when Antolini informs him that he has had lunch with Mr. Caulfield and shares the father's concern that "you're riding for some kind of a terrible, terrible fall." The professor tries intellectually to check the boy's self-destructive tendencies, as Phoebe does in her quite different way. Antolini puts the boy to bed on a couch in the living room, and says "Good night, handsome." Later Holden wakens to find "something on my head, some guy's hand." "Shaking like a madman," he concocts an excuse to leave and spends the rest of the night sleeping on a bench in Grand Central Station. "I think," he writes, "I was more depressed than I ever was in my whole life."

Although initially Holden interprets Antolini's caress as a sexual advance, in the morning he has doubts, "I mean I wondered if just maybe I was wrong about thinking he was making a flitty pass at me." Whatever his intentions, sexual or paternal, Antolini sets off the not unusual homosexual panic of adolescents. But Holden's problem is not primarily sexual. He cannot connect with anyone in any way until the burden of Allie's death is lifted.

Alone, depressed, he walks up Fifth Avenue in the morning looking for the two nuns—looking for mother—when something "very spooky" happens. "Every time I came to the end of a block and stepped over the goddam curb, I had this feeling that I'd never get to the other side of the street. I thought

I'd just go down, down, down, and nobody'd ever see me again." Once more he is at the cliff, and there is no one to catch him, to keep him from going "down, down, down"—except Allie. He cries out, "Allie, don't let me disappear."

Holden has at last touched bottom, although he is not to be spared further indignities, some of his own making. Never again will he summon Allie, which means that he begins to turn from the past and death and to move into the present and toward the living. The inevitable fantasy that he creates in moments of crisis subtly changes. He plans to go "out West, where it was very pretty and sunny and nobody'd know me." When Holden proposes to Sally that they run off to Vermont or Massachusetts, the flight is in the direction of Maine, where Allie died. In going west he moves toward the living, for D.B. is in Hollywood. Still damaged and still hungering for security, he pictures himself as a deaf mute working at a filling station and—most important—married to another deaf mute. "If we had any children," he declares, with obvious reference to his own lot, "we'd hide them somewhere. We could buy them a lot of books and teach them how to read and write by ourselves." At last Holden's locked world is opening up.

He goes to Phoebe's school to say good-by and to return her Christmas money. He is upset to find "Fuck you" scrawled on a wall, no doubt more upset than the kids who share neither his naive ideas of purity, despite his verbal profanities, nor his fears of sexuality. While he waits for Phoebe at the museum, two boys ask the way to the mummies. As Holden leads them to the Egyptian room, he begins to repeat the information given in his history examination at Pencey Prep about the process of preservation, and frightens the lads who do not share his obsession with death. Instead of a savior or a catcher, Holden turns out to be a bogey man—as unfeeling as the unfeeling adults who have never understood him. Alone in the tomb, he is mocked again by the ugly epithet of sexual assault which he finds on the walls. Typically he overreacts and at the same time punishes himself as he pictures his tombstone: Holden Caulfield—"Fuck you."

If this debasement is not enough, he suddenly has diarrhea, and passes out on the floor of a toilet. It is as though he must experience an elemental purging—get all the "crap" out of his distorted picture of life and himself. Compulsively he creates still another fantasy of flight. This time he is a thirty-five-year-old man living by himself: "I even started picturing how it would be when I came back. I knew my mother'd get nervous as hell and start to cry and beg me to stay home and not get back to my cabin, but I'd go anyway." If he is still punishing his mother—and himself—at least he pictures himself alive and at the middle of the journey.

When Phoebe comes to the museum with her luggage because she plans to go West too, once again she reaches out to her brother. The act of love is almost too much for Holden. "I got sort of dizzy and I thought I was going to pass out or something again." But he does not fall or pass out. Instead like the loved-hated parents or like a protective older brother—in short like all the other adults—he automatically advances all the sensible reasons why Phoebe's plans are "crazy." When he begins genuinely to think of someone else's lot, he assumes responsibility. He is no longer the kid who needs and demands everybody's attention.

When Phoebe proves stubborn, he returns her gift of love with another gift. He escorts her to Central Park, not to the duck pond—with its associations with death—but to the carrousel. "When she was a tiny little kid, and Allie and D.B. and I used to go to the park with her, she was mad about the carrousel." In the bedroom Holden and Phoebe had danced together like two kids, but at the carrousel Holden refuses to ride with her and watches her reach for the gold ring. In turn, when he promises to go home with Phoebe, he delights her and at the same time achieves the goal hinted at on the first page of his narrative: "I felt so damn happy all of a sudden, the way old Phoebe kept going around and around. I was damn near bawling. I felt so damn happy."

In the epilogue, Chapter 26, Holden writes of himself at age seventeen in an institution near Hollywood, not far from D.B. After a period of rest and therapy there has been no fabulous transformation, although there has been change. His language is no longer negative, nor is his attitude. He is not sure that he is going to apply himself when he returns to school in September: "I *think* I am, but how do I know? I swear it's a stupid question." Although he has to put up token resistance—after all, he is Holden Caulfield—he is ready to go "around and around" in the game of life and no longer needs Allie's mitt or hat to protect him. Nor must he picture himself as the victim of insensitive adults; the psychoanalyst's advice is not "bull."

When D.B. asks him about "all the stuff I just finished telling you about," he replies truthfully, without a defensive wisecrack. "About all I know is, I sort of *miss* everybody I told about." At last he cuts through his "crap," his evasions and hostile defenses. He wants, as he has always wanted, to establish connections, and he is well on his way to doing just that, for in his narrative he has at least established connections with readers.

"Don't ever tell anybody anything," he writes at the conclusion; "if you do, you start missing everybody." But telling is precisely what he has been doing and in the process Holden has finished mourning. Allie now rests in peace.

ALAN NADEL

Rhetoric, Sanity, and the Cold War: The Significance of Holden Caulfield's Testimony

If, as it has been widely noted, *The Catcher in the Rye* owes much to *Adventures of Huckleberry Finn*, it rewrites that classic American text in a world where the ubiquity of rule-governed society leaves no river on which to flee, no western territory for which to light out. The territory is mental, not physical, and Salinger's Huck spends his whole flight searching for raft and river, that is, for the margins of his sanity. A relative term, however, "sanity" merely indicates conformity to a set of norms, and since rhetorical relationships formulate the normative world in which a speaker functions, a fictional text—whether or not it asserts an external reality—unavoidably creates and contains a reality in its rhetorical hierarchies, which are necessarily full of assumptions and negations. This aspect of fiction could not be more emphasized than it is by Holden Caulfield's speech, a speech which, moreover, reflects the pressures and contradictions prevalent in the cold war society from which it was forged.

I   Caulfield's Speech

An obsessively proscriptive speaker, Caulfield's essay-like rhetorical style—which integrates generalization, specific examples, and consequent rules—

From *Centennial Review* 32, no. 4 (Fall 1988). © 1988 *The Centennial Review*.

prevails throughout the book, subordinating to it most of the description, narration, and dialogue by making them examples in articulating the principles of a rule-governed society. In one paragraph, for example, Caulfield tells us that someone had stolen his coat (example), that Pencey was full of crooks (generalization), and that "the more expensive a school is, the more crooks it has" (rule). In a longer excerpt, from Chapter 9, we can see how the details Caulfield sees from his hotel window—"a man and a woman squirting water out of their mouths at one another"—become examples in a series of generalizations, rules, and consequent evaluations:

> The trouble was, [principle] that kind of junk is sort of fascinating to watch, even if you don't want it to be. For instance, [example] that girl that was getting water squirted all over her face, she was pretty good-looking. I mean that's my big trouble. [generalization] In my *mind*, I'm probably the biggest sex maniac you ever saw. Sometimes [generalization] I can think of *very* crumby stuff I wouldn't mind doing if the opportunity came up. I can even see how it might be quite a lot of fun, [qualification] in a crumby way, and if you were both sort of drunk and all, [more specific example] to get a girl and squirt water or something all over each other's face. The thing is, though, [evaluation] I don't *like* the idea. It [generalization] stinks, if you analyze it. I think [principle arrived at deductively through a series of enthymemes] if you really don't like a girl, you shouldn't horse around with her at all, and if you *do* like her, then you're supposed to like her face, and if you like her face, you ought to be careful about doing crumby stuff to it, [specific application] like squirting water all over it.

Caulfield not only explains his world but also justifies his explanations by locating them in the context of governing rules, rendering his speech not only compulsively explanatory but also authoritarian in that it must demonstrate an authority for *all* his statements, even if he creates that authority merely through rhetorical convention.

With ample space we could list all the rules and principles Caulfield articulates. Here are a few: it's really hard to be roomates with people if your suitcases are better than theirs; "grand" is a phony word; real ugly girls have it tough; people never believe you; seeing old guys in their pajamas and bathrobes is depressing; don't ever tell anybody anything, if you do you start missing everybody. We could easily find scores more, to prove the book a virtual anatomy of human behavior. The book, however, also anatomizes

Caulfield's personal behavior: he lies; he has a great capacity for alcohol; he hates to go to bed when he's not even tired; he's very fond of dancing, sometimes; he's a pacifist; he always gets those vomity kind of cabs if he goes anywhere late at night, etc.

As the author of the two anatomies, Caulfield thus manifests two drives: to control his environment by being the one who names and thus creates its rules, and to subordinate the self by being the one whose every action is governed by rules. To put it another way, he is trying to constitute himself both as subject and as object; he is trying to read a social text and to write one. When these two drives come in conflict, there are no options left.

Although reified in the body of Holden Caulfield—a body, like the collective corpus of Huck and Jim, that longs for honesty and freedom as it moves more deeply into a world of deceit and slavery—this lack of options reveals an organization of power which deeply reflects the tensions of post-WWII America from which the novel emerged. The novel appeared in 1951, the product of ten years' work. Especially during the five years between the time Salinger withdrew from publication a 90-page version of the novel and revised it to more than double its length, the "cold war" blossomed.

Richard and Carol Ohmann have related *Catcher*'s immense success to the political climate of the Cold War by trying to show that Caulfield provides a critique of the phoniness "rooted into the economic and social arrangements of capitalism and their concealment." Although they tend, unfortunately, to oversimplify both the text and the relationship between literature and history, *Catcher* may indeed reveal what Fredric Jameson has termed the political unconscious, a narrative in which "real social contradictions, unsurmountable in their own terms, find purely formal resolution in the aesthetic realm." As we shall see, Caulfield not only speaks the speech of the rule contradictions embedded in the voice of his age but also displaces it by internalizing it. He thus converts his rhetoric into mental breakdown and becomes both the articulation of "unspeakable" hypocrisy and its critic. Finally, he becomes, as well, for his audience a sacrificial escape from the implications of such an articulation.

II   The Search for Phonies

Victor Navasky describes the cold war as a period having

> three simultaneous conflicts: a global confrontration between rival imperialisms and ideologies, between capitalism and Communism . . . a domestic clash in the United States between hunters and hunted, investigators and investigated . . . and,

> finally a civil war amongst the hunted, a fight within the liberal
> community itself, a running battle between anti-Communist
> liberals and those who called themselves progressives. . . .

These conflicts took not only the form of the Korean War but also of
lengthly, well-publicized trials of spies and subversives, in ubiquitous loyalty
oaths, in Senate (McCarthy) and House (HUAC) hearings, in Hollywood
and academic purges, and in extensive "anti-Communist" legislation. Even
three years before Senator Joseph McCarthy's infamous speech alleging 57
Communists in the State Department, President Truman had created a
Presidential Commission on Employee Loyalty and the Hollywood Ten had
been ruined by HUAC. Constantly, legislation, hearings, speeches and
editorials warned Americans to be suspicious of phonies, wary of associates,
circumspect about their past, and cautious about their speech. A new mode
of behavior was necessary, the President's Commission noted, because
America was now confronted with organizations which valorized duplicity:
"[these organizations] while seeking to destory all the traditional safe-guards
erected for the protection of individual rights are determined to take unfair
advantage of these selfsame safe-guards."

   Since uncovering duplicity was the quest of the day, in thinking
constantly about who or what was phony, Caulfield was doing no more than
following the instructions of J. Edgar Hoover, the California Board of
Regents, *The Nation*, the Smith Act, and the Hollywood Ten, to name a very
few. The President's Loyalty Commission, for example, announced as its
purpose both to protect the government from infiltration by "disloyal
persons" and to protect loyal employees "from unfounded accusations." The
Commission's dual role, of course, implied dual roles for all citizens: to be
protected *and* exonerated. Partly because each citizen was both the threat and
the threatened. Because the enemy was "subversive," furthermore, one could
never know whether he or she had been misled by an enemy pretending to
be a friend; without a sure test of loyalty, one could not sort the loyal from
the disloyal and therefore could not know with whom to align. The
problem—elevated to the level of national security and dramatized most
vividly by the Hiss case—was to penetrate the duplicity of phonies.

   This problem manifests itself in Caulfield's rhetoric not only in his
diatribe against "phonies" but also through a chronic pattern of signifiers
which indicate the truthfulness of Caulfield's testimony. He regularly marks
his narration with such phrases as "it (he, she, I, they) really does (do, did,
didn't, was, wasn't, is, isn't, can, had, am)," "if you want to know the truth,"
"I (I'll, I have to) admit (it)," "if you really want to know," "no (I'm not)
kidding," "I swear (to God)," "I mean it." The word "really" additionally

appears at least two dozen more times in the narration, often italicized. These signifiers, along with those which emphasize the intensity of an experience (e.g. "boy!") or the speaker's desire for clarity (e.g. "I mean. . . . ") make Caulfield's speech one which asserts its own veracity more than once for every page of narration.

Because it is so important to Caulfield that the reader not think he is a phony, he also constantly provides ample examples and illustrations to prove each assertion, even his claim that he is "the most terrific liar you ever saw in your life." Examples of such rhetorical performances abounded in the media during the novel's five-year revision period. Like many of the ex-Communist informers of the period, Caulfield's veracity rests on the evidence of his deceitfulness. This paradox is especially foregrounded by a discussion Caulfield has on the train with Mrs. Morrow, the mother of another boy at Pencey. In that discussion, he convinces the reader of his truthfulness with the same signifier he uses to make Mrs. Morrow believe his lies. Although Caulfield feels her son, Ernie, is "doubtless one of the biggest bastards that ever went to Pencey," he tells her, "'He adapts himself very well to things. He really does. I mean he really knows how to adapt himself.'" Later he adds: "'It really took everybody quite a while to get to know him.'" Having used "really" as a false signifier, Caulfield in confessing to the reader italicizes part of the word: "Then I *real*ly started chucking the old crap around." The evidence which follows should convince the reader that the italicized "real" can be trusted, so that the more he demonstrates he has duped his fellow traveler, the more the reader can credit the veracity of the italicized "real." The *real* crap is that Ernie was unaminous choice for class president but wouldn't let the students nominate him because he was too modest. Thus Caulfield proves his credibility to the reader: he *is* a good liar, but when he italicizes the "real" he can be trusted. In trying to convince Mrs. Morrow, however, he adds, "'Boy, he's *really* shy,'" and thus destroys the difference between italicized and unitalicized signifier.

III   The Meaning of Loyalty

Although presented as a trait of Caulfield's character formalized in his speech, these inconsistencies reflect as well the contradictions inherent in a society plagued by loyalty oaths. Swearing that something is true doesn't make it true, except at the expense of anything not-sworn-to. There exists, in other words, some privileged set of "true" events marked by swearing. The swearing, of course, marks them not as true but as important to the speaker— the things that he or she wants the audience to believe, cares about enough to mark with an oath. In this way, Caulfield creates a rhetorical contract—the appeal to ethos—which legitimizes the discourse. It does so, however, at the cost of all items not stipulated: they reside in the margins by virtue of being so obvious that they can be taken for granted or so unimportant that they need not be substantiated. Thus grouped together as the "unsworn," the taken-for-granted and the not-*necessarily*-so become indistinguishable parts of the same unmarked set. This is exactly what, as Americans were discovering, loyalty oaths did to the concept of loyalty. For all constitutions bind those loyal to them, and the failure to take that for granted becomes the failure to grant a group constituted by a common social contract. It leaves the "we" of "We the People" without a known referent and makes it impossible to distinguish the real American from the phony—the one so disloyal that he or she will swear false allegiance, will italicize *real* commitment in order to dupe others.

Since social contracts rely upon rhetorical contracts, the problem then is one of language. But Communism according to its accusers acknowledged neither the same social nor rhetorical contracts. According to a major McCarthy witness, ex-Communist Louis Budenz, Communists often used "Aesopean" language so that, "no matter how innocent the language may seem on its face, the initiate understood the sinister underlying message." Because no court recognizes a contract binding on only one party, in dealing with those outside the social and rhetorical contracts, the traditional constitutional rules no longer applied. In his 1950 ruling upholding the Smith Act, under which eleven leaders of the American Communist Party were sentenced to prison, Judge Learned Hand indicated that when challenged by an alternative system, "Our democracy . . . must meet that faith and that creed on its merits, or it will perish. *Nevertheless*, we may insist that the rules of the game be observed, and the rules confine the conflict to the weapons drawn from the universe of discourse" [emphasis added]. Because the Communists do not function in the same universe of discourse, the same rules do not apply to them. But, as the need for loyalty tests proved, it was impossible to distinguish those for whom the rules did not apply from those for whom they did.

To do so requires a position outside the system, from which to perceive an external and objective "truth." In other words, one needs a religion, which as Wayne Booth implies is the only source of a truly reliable narrator. All other narration must establish its credibility rhetorically by employing conventions. One of Caulfield's conventions is to acknowledge his unreliability by marking specific sections of the narration as extra-reliable. As we have seen, however, marked thus by their own confessions of unreliability, Caulfield's oaths become one more series of questionable signs, indicating not reliability but its myth. Roland Barthes has astutely demonstrated that a myth is an empty sign, one which no longer has a referent but continues to function as though it did, thus preserving the status quo. The loyalty oath is such a myth in that it preserves the idea of "loyalty" called into question by its own presence, and in that it is executed at the expense of the field in which it plays—the constituted state to which the mythical loyalty is owed.

Like Caulfield's oaths, loyalty oaths in the public realm also proved insufficient. In a truly Orwellian inversion, the "true" test of loyalty became betrayal. Unless someone were willing to betray friends, no oath was credible. With the tacit and often active assistance of the entire entertainment industry, HUAC very effectively imprinted this message on the public conscience through half a decade of Hollywood purges. As has been clearly shown, investigating the entertainment industry was neither in the interest of legislation nor—as it could be argued that an investigation of the State Department was—in the interest of national security. It was to publicize the ethic of betrayal, the need to name names.

IV   The Importance of Names

If the *willingness* to name names became the informer's credential, furthermore, the *ability* to do so became his or her capital. Thus the informer turned proper nouns into public credit that was used to purchase credibility. Caulfield too capitalizes names. The pervasive capitalization of proper nouns mark his speech; he compulsively names names. In the first three chapters alone, the narration (including the dialogue attributed to Caulfield) contains 218 proper nouns—an average of nine per page. They include people, places, days, months, countries, novels, cars, and cold remedies. Many of the names, moreover, are striking by virtue of their unimportance. Does it matter if old Spencer used "Vicks Nose Drops" or read *Atlantic Monthly*? Is it important that these items are named twice? Caulfield's speech merely mirrors the convention of the Hollywood witness by demonstrating the significance of his speech lay in alacrity, not in content:

> A certain minimum number of names was necessary; those who . . . could convince HUAC counsel that they did not know the names of enough former comrades to give a persuasive performance . . . were provided with names. The key to a successful appearance . . . was the *prompt* recital of the names of a few dozen Hollywood Reds [emphasis added].

Nor was the suspicion of Hollywood one-sided. Suspected by the right of being potentially subversive, it was suspected by liberals of being inordinately self-censored. Carey McWilliams, writing in *The Nation*, in 1949, bemoans the effects of the "graylist." Intimidated out of dealing realistically with social issues, the movies, McWilliams fears, were becoming more and more phony.

Not surprisingly, Caulfield too equates Hollywood with betrayal and prostitution. The prostitute who comes to his room, furthermore, tells him she is from Hollywood, and when she sits on his lap, she tries to get him to name a Hollywood name: "'You look like a guy in the movies. You know. Whosis. *You* know who I mean. What the heck's his name?'" When Caulfield refuses to name the name, she tries to encourage him by associating it with that of another actor: "Sure you know. He was in that pitcher with Mel-vine Douglas. The one that was Mel-vine Douglas's kid brother. *You* know who I mean." In 1951, naming that name cannot be innocent, because of its associations. Douglas, a prominent Hollywood liberal (who in 1947 supported the Hollywood Ten and in 1951 distanced himself from them) was, more importantly, the husband of Helen Gahagan Douglas, the Democratic Congresswoman whom Richard Nixon defeated in the contest for the California Senate seat. Nixon's race, grounded in red-baiting, inuendos, and guilt by association, attracted national attention and showed, according to McCarthy biographer David Oshinsky, that "'McCarthyism' was not the exclusive property of Joe McCarthy."

If Caulfield is guilty by virtue of his association with Melvyn Douglas, then guilty of what? Consorting with prostitutes? Naming names? Or is it of his own hypocrisy, of his recognition, also inscribed in his rhetoric, that he hasn't told the truth in that he actually loves the movies, emulates them, uses them as a constant frame of reference. The first paragraph of the book begins "if you really want to know the truth" and ends with the sentences: "If there's one thing I can't stand, it's the movies. Don't even mention them to me." Despite this injunction, Caulfield's speech is full of them. He acts out movie roles alone and in front of others, uses them as a pool of allusion to help articulate his own behavior, and goes to see them, even when he believes they will be unsatisfactory.

This marked ambivalence returns us again to the way historical circumstances make Caulfield's speech, like all public testimony, incapable of articulating "truth" because the contradictions in the conditions of public and private utterance have become visible in such a way as to mark all truth claims "phony." In their stead come rituals of loyalty, rituals which do not manifest truth but replace it. In presenting advertised, televised, confessionals, which were prepared, written, and rehearsed, and then were performed by real-life actors, the HUAC Hollywood investigations not only replicated the movies, but they also denied the movies distance and benignity, in short their claim to artificiality. The silver (and cathode-ray) screen is everywhere and nowhere, presenting an act of truth-telling hard to distinguish from its former fabrications, stories for the screen which may or may not have been encoded, subversive messages. So too in "real life"—the viewers of these confessions may have been duped, made inadvertently to play a subversive role, followed an encoded script produced by a secret conspiracy of the sort they're used to seeing in the movies. And of course the movies *can* be believed, for if they cannot what is all the worry about? Why bother investigating the harmless? This was the mixed message of the HUAC hearings: movies were dangerous because they *could* be believed, and movies were dangerous because they *could not*. One cannot escape such a message by discovering the "truth," but only by performing the ritual that fills the space created by the impossibility of such a discovery. In this light, perhaps, Phoebe Caulfield's role in her school play should be read. When Caulfield asks her the play's name she says:

> "'A Christmas Pageant for America'. It stinks but I'm Benedict Arnold. I have practically the biggest part . . . It starts out when I'm dying. This ghost comes in on Christmas Eve and asks me if I'm ashamed and everything. You know. For betraying my country and everything. . . . "

The passage accurately summarizes the ideal HUAC witness. The former traitor now starring in a morality play that honors the state through a form of Christian ritual, the goal of which is not the discovery of truth, but the public, "educational" demonstration of loyal behavior, in which the fiction's paragon of innocence and the nation's historical symbol of perfidy validate one another by exchanging roles.

V   Simple Truth and the Meaning of Testimony

Phoebe's play unites the two central loci for phonies in Caulfield's speech, the worlds of entertainment and of education. In questioning the phoniness of all the schools and teachers he has seen, Caulfield again articulates doubts prevalent in the public consciousness, especially as he is most critical of the Eastern Intellectual Establishment. That establishment, with Harvard as its epitome, came to represent for the readers of *Time*, for example, a form of affluence and elitism that could not be trusted. In their education section, the week of June 5, 1950, for example, *Time* quoted I. A. Richards at length on college teaching:

"You are never quite sure if you are uttering words of inspired . . . aptness, or whether you are being completely inept. Often you will find yourself incompetent enough to be fired at once if anybody was intelligent enough to see you as you are. . . .

"'Am I, or am I not, a fraud?' That is a question that is going to mean more and more to you year by year. At first it seems agonizing; after that it becomes familiar and habitual."

Again we have the same confessional paradigm. Richards gains credibility by confessing he was a fraud. He also suggests an encoded language meant to deceive the average person—anybody *not* "intelligent enough to see you as you are"; by implication, those who *were* intelligent enough participate in the conspiracy to keep the fraudulence hidden.

This issue becomes particularly germane in a period when teachers and professors were being forced to sign loyalty oaths and/or were being dismissed because of present or past political beliefs. The central issue, many faculty argued, was that academic personnel were being judged by non-academic standards. Yet Richards' statement could suggest that "true" academic standards were really a myth created by those intelligent enough to know better. Intelligence thus signified the capacity for fraud: only someone intelligent enough to see them as they are had something to hide. Because they knew more, intellectuals were more likely to know something they should confess, and not confessing hence signified probable disloyalty rather than innocence.

Time (1/23/50) made the same inferences about the psychiatrists who testified in Alger Hiss's defense, pointing out that Dr. Murray (like Dr. Binger and Hiss) was a Harvard graduate: "He backed up his colleague, Binger. Chambers . . . was a psychopathic personality. . . . He had never seen Chambers but this did not faze him. He had psychoanalyzed Adolph Hitler *in absentia*, correctly predicting his suicide."

If, filtered through *Time*'s simplifying voice, these doctors seemed foolish accomplices, Hiss himself came to stand for everything that needed exposure and rejection. About his conviction, *Time* (1/30/50) wrote: "[Hiss] was marked as a man who, having dedicated himself to Communism under a warped sense of idealism, had not served it openly but covertly; a man who, having once served an alien master, lacked the courage to recant his past, but went on making his whole life an intricate, calculated lie." Thus the past existed to be recanted, not recounted. The recounted past—the truth of one's past—became living a lie, while recanting revealed Truth, discovered not in past actions but in idealogical enlightenment, enlightenment which reveals that one's life was a lie. Analysis is intellectualized lying, *Time* had suggested in its treatment of Hiss's "authorities," part of the Intellectual conspiracy that did not revere the Truth but rather suggested that facts could be contravened by an unseen, subversive presence, knowable only to a trained elite whom the general population had to trust without evidence. For *Time*, truth was less ambiguous, existing in a transparent connection between physical phenomena and accepted beliefs, and with its authority lying outside the speaking subject. Hiss had transgressed by seeking to intervene, to analyze, to apply principles not grounded in Truth but in the trained intellect of a fallen mortal, fallen because he believed in the power of human intervention, the ability of the human intellect to discern and interpret.

This too is Caulfield's failing, and he must recognize the error of locating himself as the discoverer, interpreter and arbiter of truth and phoniness. In other words, if his speech constitutes him both as subject and object, it also constitutes him as testifier and judge, accuser and accused. It has the quality of testimony—the taking of oaths and the giving of evidence to support an agenda of charges. And like much of the most publicized testimony of its day, it has no legal status. As Navasky pointed out about the Hollywood hearings:

> [T]he procedural safeguards . . . were absent: there was no cross examination, no impartial judge and jury, none of the exclusionary rules about hearsay or other evidence. And, of course, the targets from the entertainment business had commited no crime. . . .

In such a context, it was hard to regard testimony as a form of rhetoric in a forensic argument. Although sometimes masked as such, it rarely functioned in the way Aristotle defined the concept. Rather it more often resembled testimony in the religious sense of confessing publicly one's sins. Caulfield's speech thus simultaneously seeped in conventions of both forensic testimony and spiritual, reveals the incompatability of the two, in terms of their intended audience, their intended effect, and their relationship to the speaker. Most important, forensic testimony presumes truth as something arrived at through the interaction of social and rhetorical contract, whereas spiritual testimony presumes an external authority for truth; its rhetoric *reveals* the Truth, doing so in such a way as to exempt the speech from judgment and present the speaker not as peer but as paragon.

These distinctions apply particularly to the concept of incrimination. A witness giving forensic testimony always risks self-incrimination; recognizing this, our laws allow the witness to abstain from answering questions. The paragon, who gives spiritual testimony, however, is above such self-incrimination; the paragon knows the Truth and has nothing to fear. Exercising the legal protection against self-incrimination (as many HUAC witnesses chose to do) meant the speaker was offering forensic testimony not spiritual, had thus not found the Truth, and therefore could not be trusted. Designed to protect the individual from self-incrimination, the Fifth Amendment then became the instrument of that self-incrimination. In a society that determined guilt not by evidence but by association and/or the failure to confess, people often found that the only way not to incriminate others was to claim they would be incriminating themselves. Since that claim became self-incriminating, they purchased silence by suggesting guilt. They thus internalized the dramatic conflict between social contract and personal loyalty, with the goal not of catharsis but silence. Autobiography, always potentially incriminating, had become recontextualized as testimony, but testimony itself had been freed of its evidenciary contexts and become an unbound truth-of-otherness. It potentially revealed the other—the subversive—everywhere but in the place he or she was known to be, even in the audience of investigators and/or in the speaker. The speaker, by virtue of testimony's two voices and self-incrimination's merger with its own safeguard, was as much alienated in the face of his or her own speech as in the face of his or her silence.

VI   The Case for Silence

The battle waged internally by so many during the Cold War, between spiritual and forensic testimony, public and personal loyalty, recounting and recanting, speech and silence, created a test of character. No matter how complex and self-contradictory the social text, the individual was supposed to read it and choose correctly. This is exactly the dilemma Caulfield's speech confronts from its first words:

> If you really want to hear about it, the first thing you'll probably want to know is where I was born, and what my lousy childhood was like, and how my parents were occupied and all before they had me, and all that David Copperfield kind of crap, but I don't feel like going into it, if you want to know the truth. In the first place, that stuff bores me, and in the second place, my parents would have about two hemorrhages apiece if I told anything pretty personal about them.

Caulfield will try to tell the truth to this "hearing" without incriminating himself or his parents. But at every turn he fails, constantly reflecting rather than negotiating the contradictions of his world. Against that failure weighs the possible alternative, silence, in the extreme as suicide. The memory of James Castle's suicide haunts the book. Castle, the boy at Elkton Hills, refused to recant something he had said about a very conceited student, and instead commited suicide by jumping out a window. Caulfield too contemplated suicide in the same manner after the pimp, Maurice, had taken his money and hit him. This image of jumping out the window not only connects Caulfield with Castle but also epitomizes the fall from which Caulfield, as the "catcher in the rye," wants to save the innocent.

The image of jumping out the window also typified, as it had during the stock market crash of 1929, admission of personal failure in the face of unnegotiable social demands. In 1948, for example, Lawrence Duggan fell or threw himself from the window of his New York office. Immediately Congressman Karl Mundt announced the cause was Duggan's implication in a Communist spy ring; along with five other men, his name had been named at a HUAC meeting. The commitee would disclose the other names, Mundt said, "as they jump out of windows."

On April 1, 1950, F. O. Matthiessen, "at the time," in the words of William O'Neill, "the most intellectually distinguished fellow traveler in America," jumped to his death from a Boston hotel window. In his suicide note, he wrote: " . . . as a Christian and a socialist believing in international peace, I find myself terribly oppressed by the present tensions." Although Matthiessen did not commit suicide solely for political reasons, for the general public his death symbolized the culpability and weakness of the Eastern Intellectual Establishment. His powerful intellect, his political leanings and, especially, his longstanding affliation with Harvard identified him clearly as the kind of analytic mind that typified the intellectual conspiracy *Time*, Joseph McCarthy, et al. most feared and despised. Like Hiss, he was led astray by his idealism which, in true allegorial fashion, led to deceit and ultimately the coward's way out. *Or:* like many dedicated progressives, he was hounded by witch hunters forcing him to choose between the roles of betrayer and betrayed, and leading him ultimately to leap from melodrama into tragedy. Hero or coward, Christ or Judas—in either case, in the morality drama of his day, he graphically signified the sort of fall from innocence against which Caulfield struggles.

But, in the end, Caulfield renounces this struggle, allowing that one cannot catch kids: " . . . if they want to grab for the gold ring, you have to let them do it *and not say anything*. If they fall off, they fall off, *but it's bad if you say anything to them*" [emphasis added]. Thus the solution to Caulfield's dilemma becomes renouncing speech itself. Returning to the condition of utterance, stipulated in his opening sentence, which frames his testimony, he says in the last chapter—"If you want to know the truth . . . ," this time followed not with discourse but with the recognition that he lacks adequate knowledge for discourse: " . . . I don't *know* what I think about it." From this follows regret in the presence of the named names:

> I'm sorry I told so many people about it. About all I know is, I sort of *miss* everybody I told about. Even old Stradlater and Achley, for instance. I think I even miss goddam Maurice. It's funny. Don't ever tell anybody anything. If you do, you start missing everybody.

These last sentences of the book thus replace truth with silence. The intermediary, moreover, between Caulfield's speech—deemed unreasonable—and his silence is the asylum, and we could say that the whole novel is speech framed by that asylum. It intervenes in the first chapter, immediately after Caulfield asks "if you want to know the truth" and in the last, immediately before he says he does not know what to think. In this way, the asylum functions in the manner Foucault has noted—not to remove Caulfield's guilt but to organize it "for the madman as a consciousness of himself, and as a non reciprocal relation to the keeper; it organized it for the man of reason as an awareness of the Other, a therapeutic intervention in the madman's existence."

> Incessantly cast in this empty role of unknown visitor, and challenged in everything that can be known about him, drawn to the surface of himself by a social personality silently imposed by observation, by form and mask, the madman is obliged to objectify himself in the eyes of reason as the perfect stranger, that is, as the man whose strangeness does not reveal itself. The city of reason welcomes him only with this qualification and at the price of this surrender to anonymity.

In this light, we can see that the asylum not only frames Caulfield's speech but also intervenes throughout as an increasing awareness of his otherness, marked by such phrases as "I swear to God, I'm a madman." Given the novel's frame, it is not astonishing that Caulfield's speech manifests traits of the asylum. In that his speech also manifests the contradictions of McCarthyism and the Cold War, the novel more interestingly suggests that the era in many ways institutionalized traits of the asylum. To prove the validity of his "madman" oaths, Caulfield again must assume the dual roles of subject and object, for as Foucault demonstrates, the intervention of the asylum (and, by extension we can say the Cold War) functioned by three principal means: perpetual judgment, recognition by the mirror, and silence.

A. ROBERT LEE

"Flunking Everything Else Except English Anyway": Holden Caulfield, Author

Few self-accounts, whether autobiography or novel, display quite so take-it-or-leave-it a bravura as *The Catcher in the Rye*. From Holden's opening disparagement of his early childhood as "all that David Copperfield kind of crap" through to his last, peremptory "That's all I'm going to tell about," J. D. Salinger has his narrator sound the very model of skepticism about whether indeed we do "really want to hear about it." Yet given the book's spectacular popularity since its publication in 1951, clearly only the most obdurate of readers have proved resistant to "hearing about it" and to Holden's different virtuoso flights of scorn or dismay or selective approval. For however we have come to think of Holden Caulfield—as one of the classic isolates of modern times, as the savvy but endlessly vulnerable wittiness to crassness and bad faith, as postwar American adolescence itself even—still another figure presses out deep from within. At virtually every turn Holden gives notice of his endemic and unremitting will to a style of his own, to writerliness, to showing himself, knowingly or not, as nothing less than the very author in waiting of *The Catcher in the Rye*.

In part, this identity inevitably has something to do with Salinger's originality in conceiving as his narrator the seventeen-year-old who hovers dauntingly at "six foot two and a half," whose hair has turned its celebrated and premature gray on the right side of his head, and who writes of Pencey

From *Critical Essays on Salinger's The Catcher in the Rye*, ed. Joel Salzberg. © 1990 Joel Salzberg.

Prep and his all but Lost Weekend in New York from a West Coast psychiatric ward in the wake of his nervous breakdown. But, to use a key term from the novel, the "composition" Holden puts before us offers anything but the merely offbeat recollections of a put-upon and precocious teenager. This "composition" is the latest in a career that time upon time has seen Holden "composing" other themes, other selves, and other identities. Each, however, has hithero been of the moment, a spontaneous if never other than highly particular creation conjured into being to meet a required part, or to win or deflect attention, or to fill up the spaces of his loneliness, or, often enough, simply to make good on his sheer creative overdrive. Whatever the occasion, these made-up identities are for the most part extraordinarily affecting and often wickedly funny, a kind of inspired ventroliquy on Holden's part, and at the same time a set of rehearsals, a repertoire, to be called back into play by the eventual author-autobiographer.

In this connection, too, it does not surprise that nearly all the values and people Holden most prizes possess a humanity marked out by style, by an authenticity not only of the heart and senses, but also of art. Indeed, these people are like Holden himself—the Holden who can be wilful, contrary, often impossible, yet in a manner insistently of his own making and at odds with whatever he deems dull or conformist. Each "phony," "and all," and "crumby," is reiterated as often as needed to install his own special signature as writer or monologist, a signature that would be impossible to think anybody's but his alone.

The Catcher in the Rye, as often enough noted, does indeed thereby yield a portrait of the artist, but one that, more than other comparable narratives, operates within its own rules. For a start it makes Holden's every authorial tic and habit as much an equal part of the narration as all the supposedly actual events being unfolded. One thinks not only of his use of "phony" and the like but also of the jibes at his own expense: "I'm the most terrific liar you ever saw. It's awful." He automatically assumes that he has the reader's ear: "She's all right. You'd like her," he says, notably, of Phoebe, and in almost the same phrase, of Allie. And in his off-hand way he makes frequent and meanly well-targeted judgments: "Pencey was full of crooks" or "That guy Morrow was about as sensitive as a goddam toilet seat." Holden seems, ostensibly to tell the one story that bears on "this madman stuff" only to reveal himself, fugitively, in the margins as it were, also telling another, that in which he writes himself imaginatively into being. Both stories are told by the ultimately larger self of Holden as author, the Holden who can editorialize gloriously, fire off opinions, imitate screen celebrities or his fellow preppies, and even, as it appears, brazenly flaunt his resentment at all the unlooked-to burdens of writing autobiography. But if any one overwhelming clue can be said to indicate his essential vocation, it has to do with his strongest and most symptomatic fear, that of disappearing, be it in crossing Route 202 to see "old Spencer" or Manhattan's Fifth Avenue as he talks to the dead Allie. At the very moment of making that fear articulate, transposing it from life into narrative, it is actually being dissolved and conquered.

Analogies have been much proposed for *Catcher*, particularly Dicken's *David Copperfield*, Twain's *Huckleberry Finn* and Joyce's *Portrait*. Each novel, as a life, a rite of passage, or journey, offers clear similarities in terms of type and situation. But Salinger's novel belongs still more precisely to the company of those fictional autobiographies which show their protagonists discovering their truest being in the call to authorship and in the "self" they see themselves shaping as the words precariously, yet inevitably, take sequence upon the page. Memorable as each is, Copperfield, Huck, and Dedalus tell their stories from positions of retrospect (even Copperfield with his teasing "Whether I shall turn out to be the hero of my own life . . . these pages must show"). Holden is altogether more extemporaneous, his account more volatile and rapid, or so Salinger persuades us to feel. Holden's essential styling of things—his every transition, dissolve, off-the-cuff commentary, and wisecrack—could hardly fail to implicate us from first to last in the heady business whereby as for the first time and in the mirror of his own "composition" he sees himself as whole and clear. In no way can he ever disappear again, even if he does "sort of *miss* everybody I told about."

To some extent an experiment like Gertrude Stein's *The Autobiography of Alice B. Toklas*, Stein's invention of herself through the persona of her Paris companion and memoirist, bears a resemblance to *The Catcher in the Rye*. Yet Stein's modus operandi never wholly frees itself of the suspicion of staginess or formula. Two other American first-person classics, Ralph Ellison's *Invisible Man* and *The Autobiography of Malcolm X*, however, unlikely as they might at first perhaps be thought, come closer. Both, in an overall sense, obviously tell a more consequential story than Holden's, that of the black American odyssey as against the turnings of white borgeois New York and its satellite outposts in New Jersey and Pennsylvania. But they do so in a manner and with an improvisational daring greatly of a kind. Each depicts a self, in the face of historic denial, discovering itself as it goes along, a self that, as it moves from blank to identity, marginality to center, does so as though exhilarated and even astonished at its own formulation in writing.

No one would suggest Holden to be some exact fellow traveller of Ellison's black underground "spook" or the oratorical whirlwind who becomes Malcolm X. But the story he offers in *The Catcher in the Rye* delineates a figure who equally, and equally powerfully, draws the energies of self-discovery into his own narrative. This drama of self-inscription, if we can call it so, in and of itself thereby becomes the parallel of all Holden's other doings at Pencey and in Manhattan. Not the least part of it, furthermore, is that whatever Holden's protestations to the contrary, his is a finished autobiography, a story posing as a fragment as may be but wholly complete in its beginning, middle, and end. It would do less than justice to who he is, or at least to who and what he has become, and to Salinger behind him, to think otherwise.

Holden, then, takes the writer's life out of several kinds of necessity. Despite the contrariness of his signing-off—"I'm sorry I told so many people about it"—his "composition" represents nothing less than a path to psychological health. He has, so to speak, remade himself. Moreover, the privileges of authorship, in addition, have given him his occasion as for the first time to elicit pattern, order, from what throughout his troubled young life has overwhelmingly been flux and loss. Writing, too, has ended his isolation by giving him access to a community that will read and respond to him. Above all, he has achieved his apotheosis, that of an artist writing from the fullest wellsprings of his being and so "unprostituted"—the jokily risqué term he uses about his Hollywood screenwriter brother, D.B. He has made one world into another, one prior self or circle of selves into another. Acknowledging the "author" in Holden thus becomes a critical necessity if we are to get anything like the full measure of both the tale he tells and of himself as teller.

II

From start to finish Holden qualifies as a "performing self," in Richard Poirier's phrase, "authorly" to a degree in how he sets up terms and conditions for his story. Nowhere does he do so more cannily than in the opening of *Catcher*, where his mock brusqueness in saying what he *won't* do— "I'm not going to tell you my whole goddam autobiography or anything"— and his equally mock doubts about any readerly good faith we might be assumed to possess—"If you really want to hear about it"—combine not so much to put us off as positively to command our attention. "Where I was born," "my lousy childhood," and "anything pretty personal" about his absentee parents are to be withheld, though not, apparently, the happenings behind this "madman stuff" and his being "pretty run down." How better, it could be asked, to stir curiosity or lay down guidelines as to what is to follow? His every denial and insistence betrays the "authorly" Holden, a narrator about his duties with all the animus of one who can do nothing to stop the story-telling impulses within him.

D.B., the brother who "used to be just a regular writer" but who on

Holden's estimate is "being a prostitute" in Hollywood, similarly helps to position Holden as author. D.B. has forfeited this "regularity" for the movies, for the Jaguar, and, we learn at the end, for "this English babe" who comes with him to visit Holden. But he once wrote "this terrific book of short stories" whose title piece, "The Secret Goldfish," Holden has taken to because it delineates a body of private feeling strongly held—that of "this little kid that wouldn't let anybody look at his goldfish because he'd bought it with his own money." As narcissistic as the "kid" may be, he has made of the goldfish a thing of his own, an icon or even artwork. D.B. also points ahead to remind us that Holden comes from a family of writers, not only himself as the Hollywood "prostitute" but Allie who wrote poems on his baseball mitt and Phoebe who composes her "Old Hazle Weatherfield" detective stories. All the Caulfield siblings, in fact, are compulsive fabulists, imaginers.

A number of selective highlightings, first from the Pencey scenes and then those in New York, will help unravel the rest of the pattern. The interview with "old Spencer" has rightly been admired as a comic tour de force, from the "ratty old bathrobe" worn by Spencer and the Vicks Nose Drops through to "the terrific lecture" about "Life is a game" and the dazzlingly awful nose-picking. As a parody of dead rhetoric and set-piece counseling, the episode works to perfection. But in addition to the comedy, it also serves to open up another round of perspectives on Holden as author. Whatever else Holden has failed, he has "passed English," or, as he says in his note added to the exam answer written for Spencer on the Egyptians, "It is all right if you flunk me though as I am flunking everything else except English anyway." A boy who can wonder where the ducks in Central Park go in the winter or see through received cliché—"Game, my ass. Some game"— might well "pass English." In the first instance he is about the search for some kind of benign spiritual principle and in the second about the quest for a language untrammeled by inertness or mere hand-me-down phrasing. He seeks an "English" that expresses him, his situation, not that of "phony" institutionalism.

Little wonder, then, that Holden also shows himself as a virtually insatiable reader. If he can "act out" his contrition for Spencer, assuage the history teacher's need to play the sentorian, he has books in plenty to draw upon. Not only has he been exposed to "all that Beowulf and Lord Randal My Son stuff," but to a literary syllabus as extensive as it is various. *David Copperfield* he brings into play in his first sentence. Clad in his red hunting hat while rooming with Stradlater he reads Isak Dinesen's *Out of Africa*—"I wouldn't mind calling this Isak Dinesen up." Within a trice he adds to the roster Ring Lardner, Somerset Maugham, and Thomas Hardy—"I like that

Eustacia Vye." On the train to New York he delivers himself of his thoughts on "those dumb stories in a magazine," obviously no fan of tabloid popular culture. The sex book he has read at Whooton, "lousy" as he thinks it with its view "that a woman's body is like a violin and all," comes pressingly to mind as he waits for his prostitute at the Edmont Hotel. He delivers himself about his views of the Bible—"I like Jesus and all . . . " but the Disciples " . . . were about as much use to Him as a hole in the head." With the nuns Thomas Hardy again comes into his mind: "you can't help wondering what a nun thinks about when she reads about old Eustacia," and *Romeo and Juliet* and *Julius Caesar.* He remembers a discussion on *Oliver Twist* in a film seen with Allie, a novel obviously familiar to him. His meeting with Carl Luce has him invoking Rupert Brooke and Emily Dickinson as, incongruously, a pair of "war" poets, and in turn Hemingway's *A Farewell to Arms* ("a phony book") and Fitzgerald's *The Great Gatsby* ("Old Gatsby, Old sport. That killed me," as his eye for style causes him to remark). For good measure, given the novel's title, he throws in Robert Burns, the writer from whose ditty he has conjured up his fantasy of himself being a catcher in the rye. All of these allusions he contrives to wear lightly, passing stopovers as might be in the passage of his own gathering imagination. In fact, they speak to him from within the community he will shortly join, that of authors and artists who have also and at every risk made over the world on their own creative terms.

A key moment in the process manifests itself in "the big favor" solicited of him by Stradlater, namely a "composition" that can be about anything "just as long as it's descriptive as hell." More than a little revealingly, Stradlater instructs him not "to stick all the commas and stuff in the right place." In part, this advice is to cover up Holden's authorship, but as Holden himself realizes only too well, it typifies how neither Stradlater nor much of the rest of Pencey has the faintest appreciation of what "English" means. The date with Jane Gallagher, who for Holden is the girl individualized by keeping her kings at the back in checkers but for Stradlater is no more than another sexual scalp, stirs in him the memory of Allie, live or dead his one dependable imaginative ally alongside Phoebe. Unsurprisingly he chooses to write about the mitt, the poems in green ink "written all over the fingers and the pocket and everywhere." Holden writes, too, "in his pajamas and bathrobe and my old hunting hat," as if he were kitted out for the job like some updated Victorian man of letters. Everything he pours into his "description," predictably, is wasted on Stradlater, flush as the athlete is with sexual conquest and with concerns a universe away from whatever Holden may have encoded about Allie's death—his traumatized night in the garage and the near self-mutilation of putting his writing hand through "all the goddam windows." "I sort of like writing," he confides, almost shyly, as though dimly aware that we have caught him about his most intimate and essential business. Authorship, whether he likes it or not, pursues him.

Literal authorship, however, is one thing. Holden also revels in "authoring" himself in other ways—as the student penitent for Spencer, as the scholar-prince and then canasta player for an uncomprehending Ackley, as the "goddam Governor's son" who prefers tap-dancing to government and then the no-holds-barred pugilist for Stradlater, and as "Rudolf Schmidt," the name he borrows from the dorm janitor to discuss Ernest Morrow with Mrs. Morrow when they part share a compartment on the train journey between Trenton and Newark.

This latter impersonation again helps establish Holden's drive to invention, his relentless and high-speed fabulation. His version of Morrow as "adaptable," "one of the most popular boys at Pencey," "original," and "shy and modest," not only plays to a fond mother's heart, but also shows Holden on a great improvisational jag, one invention barely put forth before another follows suit. His lie, too, about leaving Pencey early on account of needing an operation for a "tumor on the brain" smacks of a matching versatility of invention, alibi-ing as an art—as in turn does his excuse for not visiting the Morrows in Gloucester, Massachusetts, on account of a promise to see his grandmother in South America. He even starts reading the timetable to stop inventing or lying—"Once I get started, I can go on for hours if I feel like it. No kidding. *Hours.*" He cannot resist, too, trying on the role of "club car" roué, a man who knows his cocktails and has the chutzpah to ask Mrs. Morrow to join him. This is wit, style, ventroliquy, all to symptomatic good purpose. More "authoring," literary and otherwise, however, lies directly ahead as Holden alights at Penn Station and embarks upon his weekend tryst with New York.

III

"I'm traveling incognito," Holden tells the cab driver who takes him to the Edmont Hotel and who has to field the questions about where the ducks go when the Central Park lagoon freezes over in winter. Much as Holden gamely affects to apologize for the B-movie implications of the phrase— "When I'm with somebody that's corny, I always act corny too"—it again emphasizes his uninhibited and ever-burgeoning passion for invention. Doubtless the "loneliness" that tears at him always, together with his fear of disappearance and sheer nervous fidget, propel him more and more into these impersonations. Yet whatever their cause, they mark him as a peerless and habitual fantasist. And are they not, also, instance for instance, the contrivances of a self that as yet is truly "incognito," that of Holden as yet again the author? Each con-man routine and verbal sleight-of-hand virtually bespeaks authorship, an inventing self as well as invented selves. Is there not, even, a hint of the embryonic author in Holden's subsequent query to the cabbie about which band might be playing at the Taft or New Yorker and about joining him for a cocktail—"On me. I'm loaded"? For this is Holden as returnee Manhattanite, back for a good time, a glad-hander, knowing in the city's ways and willing to say the hell with expense. That he is also under-age to be drinking merely points up the masquerade. But who Holden truly is, here as elsewhere, indeed does lie "incognito."

Yet even *his* role-playing risks eclipse when he witnesses the routines being acted out at the Edmont. One window reveals the transvestite recomposing himself as a woman and then "looking at himself in the mirror." Holden does not fail to note that he is "all alone too." A second window exposes him to the "hysterics" of the couple squirting water in each other's mouths, with a possible third party just out of view. "Lousy with perverts" is Holden's reaction, much as he concedes that this "kind of junk is sort of fascinating to watch." But mere voyeur Holden is not. He wants, indeed needs, to be in the action, the absolute participant observer. To watch this urban cabaret relegates him to consumer not maker. Within a trice he is back to his own efforts, the would-be suitor to Faith Cavendish, burlesque stripper and Eddie Birdsell's "ex." Much as he fails to talk her round—"I should've at least made it for cocktails or something"—it leads him on to the person he knows to have a truly creative center, none other than his fellow writer and infant sister, Phoebe.

"Old Phoebe," Holden muses, "You never saw a little kid so pretty and smart in your whole life." But no sooner has he made an inventory of all that makes Phoebe an object of passionate fondness for him—the straight A's, the short red hair stuck behind her ears, her "roller-skate skinny" body, her ability to speak Robert Donat's lines in *The 39 Steps* and stick up a finger with part of the middle joint missing—than he also adds a detail as close as could be to his own impulses. Alongside D.B. and Allie, "a wizard," Phoebe is a writer. Holden gives the information as follows:

> Something else she does, she writes books all the time. Only, she doesn't finish them. They're all about this kid named Hazel Weatherfield—only old Phoebe spells it "Hazle." Old Hazle Weatherfield is a girl detective. She's supposed to be an orphan, but her old man keeps showing up. Her old man's always a "tall attractive gentleman about 20 years of age." That kills me. Old Pheobe. I swear to God you'd like her. . . . She's ten now, and not such a tiny kid any more, but she still kills everybody—everybody with any sense, anyway.

Holden recognizes in Phoebe not just a sister but a figure whose creative quirks amount to perfection. She cannot finish her stories. She gets her proportion all out of joint (the twenty-year-old father). The name "Hazle" is either an inspired abbreviation or a misspelling, not to say an ironic echo of Faith Cavendish's "Cawffle" for Caulfield. And she makes her detective an orphan with a parent. The logic here, of course, is that of a child's imagination, the logic of splendid fantasy more than hard fact or chronology. Holden recognizes in it the same authenticity as in D.B.'s "The Secret Goldfish" or Allie's poems in green ink, a Caulfield energy of imagination by which he, too, is wholly possessed. Nonetheless, his own "compositions" have still supposedly to take written shape, even though they are in fact being realized even as he describes Phoebe and everybody else.

His other "authoring" goes on, however, as unstoppable and fertile as ever. He tells "the three witches," Laverne, Old Marty, and Bernice, with whom he drinks and dances in the Lavender Room, that his name is "Jim Steele," that if not Peter Lorre than he has seen Gary Cooper "on the other side of the floor," and that "sometime" he will look them up in Seattle. But when, once more rebuffed, he calls to mind Jane Gallagher, it is as another literary ally, another fellow traveler in the ways of the imagination. She may well lose eight golf balls, be "muckle-mouthed," keep her kings at the back, be "terrific to hold hands with," and get hold of his neck at the movies, but she also has a redeeming affinity with "composition" and the written word. Once again Holden alights on aspects of someone else that mirror his own writerly alter ego: "She was always reading, and she read very good books. She read a lot of poetry and all. She was the only one, outside my family, that I ever showed Allie's baseball mitt to, with all the poems written on it. She'd never met Allie or anything, because that was her first summer in Maine— but I told her quite a lot about him. She was interested in that kind of stuff."

Jane belongs in a companionship of style, and Holden responds accordingly. Like D.B. before the "prostitution," Allie, and Phoebe, she recognizes and opens to the things of the imagination. Others, too, will embody this for Holden: the black piano-player at Ernie's—"He's so good he's almost corny"; the two nuns (one of whom teaches English); "this colored girl singer" Estelle Fletcher whose record of "Little Shirley Beans" he buys for Phoebe; Miss Aigletinger who took them to the Museum of Natural History; "Old James Castle" who was bold enough to tell Phil Stabile he was conceited, would not take it back, and was driven to jumping to his death at Elkton Hills school (a boy, significantly, with "wrists about as big as pencils"); and Richard Kinsella, who during "Oral Comp" always gets derided for his "digressions" (of which Holden observes, "I mean it's dirty to keep yelling 'Digression!' at him when he's all nice and excited"). Like all of these, Jane appeals to his need for alliances against the dead hand of *un*creativity and "phoniness."

His trip to Ernie's, and the Catch-22 conversation en route in which the cab driver Horwitz tries to find the logic of his question about the Central Park ducks—he unwittingly comes close with "If you was a fish, Mother Nature'd take care of *you*, wouldn't she?"—again call into play Holden's skills as literary impresario. "Old Ernie" he quickly marks down as a "phony," a mere exhibitionist rather than legitimate piano-player who is given to "putting all these dumb, show-offy ripples in the high notes, and a lot of other very tricky stuff that gives me a pain in the ass." He hates the clapping, the instant "mad" applause. He even, teasingly, thinks of himself as "a piano player or actor or something" to the effect that "I wouldn't want them to *clap* for me. . . . I'd play in the goddam closet." As if from instinct, Holden knows that good music—good writing or good art in general—needs a right, intimate, true response and not mere noise. But such surrounds him, especially when he runs into Lillian Simmons who asks him about D.B. who "went with" her for a while ("In *Ho*llywood!," she gushes, "How *mar*velous! What's he *do*ing?") Lillian he can just about tolerate, but not the "Navy guy" with her. In a last stab of invention he designates Lillian's date "Commander Blop or something."

His experiences with "the elevator guy" Maurice and Sunny might be thought a case of art outrunning life. Holden's virginity, his sex-book good manners as he thinks them when the girl gets to the room—"'How do you do,' I said. Suave as hell, boy"—his parlor-game attempt at conversation in the guise once again of "Jim Steele," and his excuse of having had an operation on his "clavichord" hovers between pathos and French farce. When Maurice returns for the rest of the money, he knows just whom he is dealing with, however—"Want your parents to know you spent the night with a whore?" "A dirty moron" Holden can call him, but he can't "act" his way out of getting slugged. What he can, and does, do, typically, is reinvent himself as a movie hero, a bleeding, tough-guy private eye. He acts out in life what he will go on to act out in his writing:

> About half way to the bathroom, I sort of started pretending I had a bullet in my guts. Old Maurice had plugged me. Now I was on the way to the bathroom to get a good shot of bourbon or something to steady my nerves and help me *really* get into action. I pictured myself coming out of the goddam bathroom, dressed and all, with my automatic in my pocket, and staggering around a little bit. Then I'd walk downstairs, instead of using the elevator. I'd hold on to the bannister and all, with this blood trickling out at the side of my mouth a little at a time. What I'd do, I'd walk down a few floors—holding on to

my guts, blood leaking all over the place—and then I'd ring the elevator bell. As soon as old Maurice opened the doors, he'd see me with the automatic in my hand and he'd start screaming at me in this very high-pitched, yellow-belly voice, to leave him alone. But I'd plug him anyway. Six shots right through his fat hairy belly. Then I'd throw my automatic down the elevator shaft—after I'd wiped off all the finger prints and all. Then I'd crawl back to my room and call up Jane and have her come over and bandage up my guts. I pictured her holding a cigarette for me to smoke while I was bleeding and all. The goddam movies. They can ruin you. I'm not kidding.

As pastiche Chandler or Hammett or Erle Stanley Gardner this would take some beating—film noir from an expert. But Holden is also "scripting" his own part, an author-director writing himself into his own text. The way ahead has once more been richly indicated.

It is so, again, in Holden's meeting with the two nuns as he awaits his link-up with "old Sally Hayes." His mind drifts effortlessly across his life present and past, Sally with her flurry of words like "grand" and "swell" and the recollection of Dick Slagle who pretended Holden's suitcases were his own at Elkton Hills (despite Holden's gesture of putting them out of sight under his bed). Slagle has taken refuge in the word "bourgeois," an intended put-down of Holden, but as tired a form of language as Sally's schoolgirlisms. In encountering the nuns, however, Holden again finds himself recharged by their evident genuineness, the one next to him especially with her "pretty nice smile," her warm thank-you for his contribution, her being an English teacher, and perhaps most of all her enthusiasm on hearing "English was my best subject." As much as he cannot resist two "digressions" of his own—on what a nun thinks about the "sexy stuff" in *The Return of the Native* or *Romeo and Juliet* and on his father's one-time Catholicism—he sees in his listeners a decency that all but humbles him. He also upbraids himself for having even to think of money in connection with them and for blowing smoke in their faces. "They were very polite and nice about it," he reports, as unfeignedly charitable about his rudeness as about not bringing "Catholicism" into the conversation. Holden writes of them as of Jane or Phoebe or the hat-check girl, women for whom one of his wilder "performances" would be wholly wrong.

Holden's next foray into a literary arena, or at least something close, arises out of his date with Sally Hayes ("the queen of the phonies") to see Alfred Lunt and Lynn Fontanne in the Broadway benefit show *I Know My Love*. No sooner does he buy the tickets than his mind takes off on "acting," the whole nature of "performance" itself. He thinks as a veteran of bad or unauthentic "performances"—those of Spencer, Stradlater, Ackley, Buddy Singer from The Lavender Room, Old Ernie, and "white girl" singers of "Little Shirley Beans," among others. The latter, who lack Estelle Fletcher's "very Dixieland and whorehouse" feel, can also be compared with the "terrific whistler" Harris Macklin and the "swell" kid he hears "singing and humming" Burns's lines "If a body catch a body coming through the rye." The child's obvious unphoniness "made me feel better." Such are his touchstones for his dislike of "acting" ("I hate actors") and his irreverent slaps at Laurence Olivier's Hamlet ("too much like a goddam general, instead of a sad, screwed-up type guy"). Holden's own touch of Hamletism also, no doubt, plays into these judgments, his own need to find out how exactly to "act" for himself. The other touchstone he turns to lies in the exhibits in the museum, "unactorly" "glass case" art that does not "move," is "warm," and is free of all the "dog crap and globs of spit and cigar butts from old men" that deface Central Park. "Performance" as seen in the museum—whether the Indians rubbing sticks or the squaw with the bosom weaving a blanket or the Eskimo fishing or the deer and birds—all strike Holden as things that "should stay they way they are," natural and "forever" as indeed exhibits in a natural history museum might be expected to be.

His verdict on the Lunts has exactly to do with their unnaturalness. They overact, or rather "didn't act like people and they didn't act like actors"; theirs are performances whose off-centeredness he rightly thinks "hard to explain." Matchingly hard for him to explain to Sally is his own "performance": his hatred of the "dopey movie actor" type he sees at the intermission and of Sally's Ivy League "buddyroo," of conversation about the Lunts as "angels," and even of Sally herself. On he persists, however, through a risingly frenetic inventory of New York, taxicabs, Madison Avenue buses, "phony guys that call the Lunts angels," and his own experience of boys' prep schools. But when he tries to "author" an alternative, Sally and himself as pastoral homesteaders in Massachusetts and Vermont, he finds himself speaking—writing—in the air, cut down by the unimaginativeness of Sally's response. Their exchange ends in disaster ("I swear to God I'm a madman"), but as he takes stock he also thinks that at the time of "writing" his script for Sally and himself "I *meant* it." Holden, once again, has become most alive and most himself in making an imagined world.

Nor does Holden find his direction from the two would-be mentors he seeks out, Carl Luce and Mr. Antolini. Both betray him, or at least fail to grasp the essential human and creative purposes behind Holden's turning to them. Luce he has been drawn to because he knows or pretends to know the mysteries of sexual life. He also has "the largest vocabulary of any boy at

Whooton" and "intelligence." But Holden suspects him from the outset of being a "flit" himself, a mere "hot shot" parader of his ego and vanity. As to Antolini, his betrayal cuts even deeper. Yet another English teacher, he has won Holden's admiration for trying to talk D.B. out of going to Hollywood and for being his "best" teacher. But he also has his not-so-hidden purposes in calling Holden "you little ace composition writer," in welcoming him to the Antolini apartment for the night, and for playing the sage with his citations from William Stekel on "brilliant and *creative* men." The game is revealed in his homosexual pass, that "something perverty" which for Holden is not only sexual but also a sell-out of all the "literary" advice he has had served up to him by Antolini. Only in Holden's *own* will to make good on the artist in himself, Saligner invites us to recognize, can lie his salvation.

The pointers in that direction are given in abundance. Holden tellingly casts his mind back to D.B.'s conversation with Allie about war writing and about Rupert Brooke, Emily Dickinson, Ring Lardner, and *The Great Gatsby*. Out in the park again looking for ducks he starts picturing "millions of jerks coming to my funeral and all." At his parents' apartment he goes into his "bad leg" routine for the new elevator boy. In Phoebe's room he experiences a near shock of recognition on reading the entries in her notebooks, one stylist's salute to another. She, in her turn, understands the broken record pieces he is carrying for her; the significance of his "I passed English"; the parable of James Castle and Holden's related "catcher" fantasy; and what they are about in dancing the "four numbers" to her radio. The "something very spooky"—his fear of disappearing on Fifth Avenue—serves to indicate the ebb before the storm, the lowest point. Not only must he erase all the "fuck you"s from the walls in order to make a world worthy of each Allie and Phoebe, he must also write himself back into being and into a health on the other side of the "dizziness" and "crazy stuff" that threatens his very existence. "Mad," euphoric, certainly, though he appears in company with Phoebe on the carrousel (that modern incarnation of a medieval art pageant) as it plays "Smoke Gets in Your Eyes" in the rain, Holden can in fact combat his fear of disappearance only through art, authorship. What greater apprenticeship, after all, could anyone have served?

"That's all I'm going to tell about" may indeed be his parting shot, but it is an "all" of whose variety, drama, or fascination, we have been left in no doubt. Only an author of his vintage, too, could offer the advice "Don't ever tell anybody anything. If you do, you start missing everybody." For in making text of life, "goddam autobiography" of experience, he has separated the observer in himself from the participant. He has become, willingly or not, the person he himself has most sought out from the beginning and who in return has most sought him out, none other than Holden Caulfield, author.

JOYCE ROWE

Holden Caulfield and American Protest

On a gray winter afternoon Holden Caulfield, frozen to the quick by more than icy weather, crosses a country road and feels he is disappearing. This image of a bleak moral climate which destroys the soul is not only the keynote of J. D. Salinger's *The Catcher in the Rye* but of much that now seems representative of the general tone of American cultural commentary in the aftermath of World War Two, when the novel was conceived. By 1951 (the year of *Catcher*'s publication) the ambiguities of the cold war, of American global power and influence, were stimulating a large popular audience to find new relevance in well-worn images of disaffection from the modern world. These, which historically had been identified with an aesthetic or intellectual elite, were increasingly being adapted to popular taste as they bore on current social and political concerns. The impact of David Riesman's classic sociological study, *The Lonely Crowd*, published one year before *Catcher*, may have paved the way for a new public concern with the disturbing subject of American character; but the immediate interest Riesman's book aroused and its relatively large sale suggest a readership already sensitized to the kind of anomie which Riesman described and from which Holden Caulfield suffers.

In a sense, Salinger's novel functions at a crossroads, a point on an aesthetic and spiritual journey that he was soon to leave behind. Not unlike the author of *David Copperfield* and *Oliver Twist*, whom he is all too anxious

From *New Essays on* the Catcher in the Rye, ed. Jack Salzman. © 1991 Cambridge University Press.

105

to mock, Salinger created a work that is rich enough in language, reference, and scene to captivate innocent and sophisticated readers alike. Indeed, it is only through the democratic nature of his audience that Salinger achieves any version of that ideal community of sensibility and response whose essential absence determines Holden's resistance to the world as it is.

Putting aside the many pleasures of authorial wit, narrative skill, and aesthetic energy that are the first fruits of a reading of *Catcher*, I want to concentrate on a perspective which, thus far, has not received any real critical scrutiny. This is Salinger's ability to infuse a rather formulaic disaffection not merely with the tormented urgency of an individual adolescent voice, but with a resonance that suggests much about the contemporary state of traditional American ideals and aspirations. Holden's brand of alienation gains in significance when viewed not only laterally, in relation to contemporary styles of resistance (as many critics have already done), but historically, in its relation to and displacement of cultural themes which had preoccupied many earlier American writers. To trace such a pattern is, I hope, to deepen our sensitivity to the role that literature plays in shaping the social and moral options that define identity in an historical culture.

Like earlier social resisters in American literature, Holden holds to his own vision of authenticity in the teeth of a morally degraded society. Unlike his forbears, however, he has little faith in either nature or the power of his dreams to compensate for what his "own environment [cannot] supply." The "perfect exhilaration" that Emerson once felt, crossing the snow puddles of Concord Common at twilight, has been transmuted in Holden's urban, modern consciousness to a puzzled speculation: periodically he "wonders" where the ducks in Central Park go in winter when the lagoon in which they live freezes over. The contrast of freezing and freedom, a keynote of Salinger's style, reminds us that the spiritual freedom traditionally symbolized by migratory birds is the remotest of possibilities for Holden. From beginning to end of his journey, from school to sanitarium, Holden's voice, alternating between obscenity and delicacy, conveys his rage at the inability of his contemporaries to transcend the corrosive materialism of modern American life. Many critics have berated him for being a rebel without a cause, asking, in Maxwell Geismar's words, "But what does he argue *for?*" But this inability to move forward and assert a positive goal would seem to be precisely the point of his character.

As a precocious but socially impotent upper-middle-class adolescent who is entirely dependent upon institutions that have failed him, Holden has none of the resources—spiritual, economic, or vocational—that might enable him to becomes Thoreau's "majority of one." In Thoreau's claim that each of us can become a sovereign unit if we act according to the dictates of conscience, we have a classic American "Antinomian" statement, in which the highest form of individualism, of true self-reliance, is to become, paradoxically, an image of the community's best self. *Walden* opens with "Economy," an account of Thoreau's expenditures for building his house, and ends with a vision of spiritual regeneration spreading through the land. In this conception, to rebuild the self is to regenerate the community. Thoreau's Antonomianism is thus not merely a private or eccentric choice but one that manages to fuse all elements of experience—aesthetic, spiritual, social, national—into a unified endeavor. All need not go to the woods, but all must live as if they had discovered Walden Pond within themselves. Although Holden, lacking faith in the power of self-regeneration, is no Thoreau, neither is his dilatory rebellion merely the measure of his own eccentricity. It too symbolizes a pervasive social failure. Like Pencey Prep, an elite boarding school full of crooks, materialist America desecrates and debases whatever falls to its care. A society that had once expressed its redemptive hopes in symbols of great moral or millenial power—Winthrop's City on the Hill, Melville's *Pequod* going down with a "living part of heaven" nailed to its mast—now finds its goals in the platitudes of "adjustment" psychology and the regenerative therapeutic of the sanitarium. What, indeed, is it *for*?

In Holden's postwar lexicon, America and the world are interchangable terms. And American global hegemony is given its due in the "Fuck you" expletives which Holden sees as an ineluctable blight spreading through space and time—from the walls of his sister's school, to the tomb of the Egyptian mummies at the Metropolitan Museum, to his own future gravestone. ("If you had a million years . . . you couldn't rub out even *half* the 'Fuck you' signs in the world.") Like Scott Fitzgerald, Salinger envisions American society as a kind of gigantic Midas, frozen at the heart and thus unable to mature. For all its wealth, its members cannot generate enough respect for their own humanity to care either for their past or their future.

But while Holden lacks the moral energy to make resistance signify as an individual action, he shares with his classic forbears (Hester Prynne, Ishmael, Jay Gatsby) an unwillingness to recognize the ambiguous truths of his own nature and his own needs. This lack of self-awareness characteristic of American heroes, this refusal to probe the tangled underbrush where psychological and social claims intertwine, leads to a familiar pattern: a sense of self-versus-world, an awareness so preoccupied with a lost ideal that any real social engagement is evaded. Thus, paradoxically, rebellion only reinforces the status quo.

Holden's evasion is embodied in a strategy familiar to those who recognize that when Huck Finn lights out for "the Territory" he is making a bid for a hopeless hope—freedom from human contingency; and that when Nick Carraway returns to the West he is following the same path to an unrepeatable past that he has consciously rejected in the pattern of Gatsby's life. Like these dreamers, Holden too is commited to a hopeless vision that makes all the more acute his disgust with the actual. But, in comparison to his forebears, Holden's ideal is a far more diminished thing. It lies in a sunlit childhood Eden, dominated by the image of his dead brother, Allie, who stands for whatever is most authentic in Holden's inner life. Unlike Gatsby, who sacrifices himself to his passion for the past, Holden cannot deceive himself: there is no resurrecting the past, because Allie is dead. This hard fact reduces what was in Gatsby a buoyant, if misguided, hope, to a barren and ineffectual nostalgia. As a mordant comment on American dreamers, it is the last twist of the knife.

Allie's death occurred when Holden was thirteen, the age when puberty begins. On Allie's side of the border it is still childhood, a time when self and world seem, at least in memory, to exist in an enchanted unity. The painful rupture of this sense of self-completion by adolescent self-consciousness and self-doubt is figured in Holden's ritual smashing of the garage window panes at the news of Allie's death. The fact that Holden breaks his own hand in the act—a kind of punitive self-sacrifice—only underscores its symbolic relation to the greater self-mutilation which the loss of childhood signifies for him. The psychic wilderness into which he falls leaves him in a state of continuous nervous anxiety—of being and belonging nowhere, of acute vulnerability to the aggressions and depredations of others against his now-diminished sense of self. But this anxiety never catalyzes any recognition of the enormity of his needs, or of the inevitable limitations of his character. By the end of the story Holden does realize that his vision of himself as catcher was only a daydream. He cannot save either himself or those he loves. ("The thing with kids is, . . . If they fall off, they fall off, but it's bad if you say anything to them.") But this hard-won insight—sustained through his feeling for his little sister Phoebe—is as close as Holden ever comes to establishing any reciprocity with others, or any awareness of the imperatives that operate in their lives.

The notion of the fall into experience as spiritual castration or social betrayal—the dark legacy of romanticism—has had particular importance for those American artists who have viewed American experience from the vantage point of the country's historic ideals. Of course, among those writers we term "classic" there are distinctions to be made. In "The May-Pole of Merry Mount" Hawthorne allegorized adulthood in terms of the marriage ritual, whereby a man and a woman, brought to moral consciousness through their feeling for one another, sublimate the primitive passions of childhood in the social responsibilities of communal life. But Hawthorne's view of the potential for human happiness in adult life (which becomes his own form of idealism) is something of an exception to the more common, albeit complex, ambivalence of nineteenth-century American writers toward the value of what Wordsworth called "the still sad music of humanity"—a melody which can be heard only by those who relinquished their longing for the intuitive glories of childhood.

Indeed, as the century wears on and industrial society assumes its characteristic modern shape, the American scene of despair at and revulsion from the norms of adult life seems to increase. Writers as diverse in sensibility, experience, and social orientation as Dreiser, Wharton, and Hemingway have created, in *Sister Carrie*, *The House of Mirth*, and *The Sun Also Rises*, works that are remarkably congruent in their protagonists' ultimate response to their world. Hurstwood, disintegrating under the pressure of his confused longings, can find solace only in the rhythmic motion of his rocking chair pulled close to the warmth of the radiator. Similarly, Lily Bart, overcome by her tortuous social battles, seeks a lost primal warmth by imagining herself cradling a baby in her arms as she relapses into a final narcoticized sleep; and Jake Barnes, made impotent by the war, is unable to imagine a way out of that no-man's-land of lost souls whose wayward pleasures postpone forever the psychosexual dilemmas of adult life. In one form or another, the regression to childhood serves as an "over-determined" response to the limitations of social and individual reality confronting these protagonists. So Holden, praying to the image of his dead brother, fights to hold on to what he fears most to have lost, struggling through a barren present peopled by Stradlaters and Ackleys—"slobs" secret or pathetically overt; moral ciphers who exploit by arrogance or by whining manipulation. The bathos of American society turns out to be the real illness from which Holden suffers. In the degree to which we respond to his voice, to the bid his apostrophes make for our allegiance, his condition of loneliness and longing becomes a mirror of our own predicament.

What Holden shares with, indeed inherits from, such classic American prototypes as the new man of Emerson's essays, the narrator of *Walden*, or of "Song of Myself," or of *Adventures of Huckleberry Finn*, is both a way of perceiving reality—a "horizon of expectations," in the words of E. H. Gombrich—and a way of speaking that enforces this view on the reader/auditor by discrediting or delimiting all potentially competing voices. Both his overt aggression and his more subtle hostility toward others are regularly redeemed by the vitality of his compassion, intelligence, and wit. The reader, like one of Holden's loyal though exasperated teachers, is continually persuaded to acknowledge Holden's innate superiority to those around him. All his conflicts seem designed to reinforce this persuasion, to bind the reader closer to him. The startling intimacy of his address, beginning with "If you really want to hear about it," but quickly becoming "You should have been there," "You would have liked it," flatters the reader by implying that he or she shares in Holden's delicacies of feeling and taste. In effect, the reader fills the space that Allie's death leaves vacant, his silent allegiance the token of an ideal communion in which Holden might find his authenticity confirmed. Indeed, Holden's idiosyncratic friendship with the reader compensates proleptically for the final loss he suffers in freeing his sister from her sacrificial loyalty to him. But such an "ideal communion," demanding nothing less than the absolute acceptance and mutual joy of his lost relations with Phoebe and Allie, leads to a profound distortion of the reciprocal norm implied in the term. By trying to convert us to his way of seeing and feeling—incorporating us, as it were, into his consciousness while distancing himself from others—Holden unconsciously makes clear that such a bond could never be the basis for the dialogic tensions, sympathies, and re-visions upon which the real community depends.

Although Holden's consciousness, like that of all first-person narrators, is the lens through which we view his world, it does not follow that the perspective which the reader shares with the narrator must be restricted as it is here. Not that Holden is so thoroughly reliable that we cannot see his own confusions and pretensions; there are obvious discrepancies between what he says about himself and the truth of his situation and feelings. His boarding school precocity masks a vulnerability to social humiliation; his pride in his looks and intelligence does little to assuage his guilty fascination with and fear of female sexuality; and his displaced aggression only underscores his doubts about his own sexual potency. But these effects are all too obvious. They exist not for the sake of challenging or complicating our empathy with Holden, but of reinforcing it by humanizing him with the same falsities and fears, the same ambiguous mix of "crumby" and decent impulses, that we can accept in ourselves. They make us like him better, believe in his innate decency as we wish to believe in our own, and so encourage us to accept his view of experience as an adequate response to the world. Indeed Holden, "confused, frightened and . . . sickened" by the behavior of others, flatters the reader's sense of his own moral acumen; it is all too easy to accept Holden as an exemplar of decency in an indecent age.

Although Holden claims that in telling his tale he has come to "miss" Ackley, Maurice, and the others, his presentation of these figures hardly suggests a deep engagement with the substance of their lives. Like Thoreau's Walden neighbors, whose prodigal habits are introduced only to reinforce the superiority of the narrator's "economy," the characters that Holden meets have little depth apart from their function as specimens of a depressingly antithetical world. If one cares about the three female tourists from Seattle with whom Holden tries to dance, it must be for the sake of one's own humanity, not theirs. They are like flies on the wall of Holden's consciousness—their own histories or motivations need not trouble us. Thus Holden's plunge into the urban muddle, while it seems to provide images of the social complexity of modern America, turns out to be a curiously homogeneous affair: each class or type merely serves as another reflection of a predetermined mental scheme. In this hall of mirrors the apparent multiplicity of experience turns out to be largely a replication of the same experience, in which those who act out of purpose, conviction, or faith are heartbreakingly rare.

In place of authenticity Holden finds an endless appetite for the glamour of appearance, for the vanity of effect and approval. The story that he writes for Stradlater about the poems on Allie's baseball mitt is rejected by his "unscrupulous" roommate because it doesn't follow the rules of the English composition assignment: "'You don't do *one damn thing* the way you're supposed to,'" says the infuriated Stradlater. "'Not one damn thing.'" Holden, of course, resists the rules in order to explore his own nascent artistic integrity, while around him those with more claim to our respect than the obtuse Stradlater betray talent and spirit alike by modeling themselves on one another and conforming their behavior to the regulations of a standardized "performance."

Ernie, the talented "colored" piano player who runs his own New York nightclub, is a case in point. He has learned to capture the attention of his customers by performing before a spotlighted mirror. His face, not his *fingers*, as Holden points out, is the focus of his style. Once very good, he now parodies himself and packs in the customers who, themselves anxiously performing for one another, applaud Ernie wildly. "I don't even think he *knows* any more when he's playing right or not," Holden says. Holden's sense of artistry thus serves as a measure of all false values. To the degree that we endorse his authenticity we, who would "puke" along with him, are enabled to share it.

Because there is no other character in the book to provide serious commentary on, or resistance to, Holden's point of view, his experience lacks the kind of dilectical opposition, or reciprocal sympathy, through which he, and we, might develop a more complex sense of the imperatives of American social reality. As he says about the abortive attempt of Mr. Spencer to focus his attention on his failed history exam: "I felt sorry as hell for him. . . . But I just couldn't hang around there any longer, the way we were on opposite sides of the pole. . . . " It is this need to polarize and abstract all personal relations that defeats any possibility of normative social connection and engagement. Though Holden complains that people "never give your message to anybody," that "people never notice anything," it is his dominating consciousness, setting himself and the reader a world apart, that insures his isolation.

Holden's continuous need to defend himself from the encroachments of others generates the verbal disguise he uses to fictionalize all his encounters with adults. The games he plays with Mr. Spencer and Mrs. Morrow, "shooting the bull," telling each what he thinks will most interest and please, enable him to distance himself from the false self his false phrases create as he attempts to protect the true core of his being. As the psychoanalyst D. W. Winnicott has described it, "the true self" is a core of identity which is always invulnerable to external reality and never communicates with it. In adolescence, "That which is truly personal and which feels real must be defended at all cost." Winnicott's description of what violation of its integrity means to the true self—"Rape and being eaten by cannibals . . . are mere bagatelles" by comparison—brings to mind the emotional horror that Hawthorne displays toward the violation of another's deepest self, which he calls the Unpardonable Sin. This sense of an integrity to be defended at all cost shapes the Antinomianism, as it does the duality, of Hester Prynne, Huck Finn, and Melville's most notable protagonists. But unlike these forbears, whose need for self-protection is clearly denoted by their double lives, Holden has very little inner or secret freedom in which to function. If society is a prison, then, as in a nightmare tale of Poe, the walls have moved inward, grazing the captive's skin.

Seen in this light, Holden's constant resort to obscenity serves as a shield, a perverse rite of purification that protects him from the meretricious speech of others, which threatens his very existence. Language, for Holden, is a moral matter. In the tradition of Puritan plain-speech, which has had such a marked influence on American prose style, the authenticity of the word derives from, as it points toward, the authenticity of the mind and heart of the speaker. But unlike the narrators of *Walden* and "Song of Myself," who give voice to a language fully commensurate with their visionary longings, Holden's imprecations and expletives ultimately serve to define his impotence; they reveal the degree to which he is already contaminated by the manners, institutions, and authorities of his society. The inadequacy of his vocabulary, upon which he himself remarks ("I have a lousy vocabulary") is a reflection not merely of his adolescent immaturity, but of the more abiding impoverishment from which he as a representative hero suffers—the inability to conceptualize any form of social reciprocity, of a reasonably humane community, in which the "true self" might feel respected and therefore safe.

Lacking such faith there is finally nothing that Holden can win the reader to but complicity in disaffection.

It is a literary commonplace that the English novel—from Austen, Dickens, and Conrad to writers of our own day, like Iris Murdoch—has regularly focused its critical energies on the interrelation of social institutions and individual character. In the work of English and European writers generally, society is the ground of human experience. Although many English protagonists enter their stories as orphans, their narratives lead toward a kind of self-recognition or social accomodation to others that represents the evolving meaning of their experience. One grows, develops, changes through interactions with others in a web of social and personal forces which is simply life itself.

But classic American heroes never make such accomodations. Their identities are shaped, not by interaction with others but in resistance to whatever *is*, in the name of a higher social, ethical, or aesthetic ideal. This, as I have noted, is the ground of their Antinomianism—a public or exemplary heroism, designed to be the only morally respectable position in the narrative. Orphanhood has functioned quite differently for American heroes than for European. More a starting point from which the hero must evolve a social and moral identity, it represents a liberation from the past that is a totalizing condition of existence—spiritual, psychological, political, and metaphysical. American heroes, seemingly alone, free, and without family or history, test the proposition that a new world might bring a new self and society into being. Although in each case the hero or heroine's effort issues in failure, there is no conventional recognition of this experiential truth on the part of the protagonist, no willingness to recalculate his or her relations to society or history. American individualism thus reshapes the archetypal pattern of the orphaned young man (or woman) seeking an adult identity by coming to terms with him or herself in the matrix of family life.

Indeed, the family, as the basis for individual as well as social identity, hardly exists in classic nineteenth-century American literature. Almost invariably American heroes lack the memory of past roots. Hawthorne's *The Scarlet Letter* is perhaps the proof text for this statement. Hester Prynne, having shed her European past, stands before the Puritan community, her infant in her arms, unwilling to identify the father—a revelation that would establish a new family (in Hester's ideal terms) on these shores. The fact that Pearl returns to Europe at the story's end, that Dimmesdale tortures himself to death rather than acknowledge his paternity, and that Hester herself remains alone, dreaming of the New World community yet to be, suggests how thoroughly discouraged this most "social" of our classic novelists was about the prospects for authentic family relations in American society.

American heroes like Ishmael and Gatsby are fatherless by choice as well as circumstance. Ishmael will continue to wander as he seaches for his lost homeland; Gatsby reaches toward an impossible transcendence whose measure lies precisely in its ineffable difference from the world he knows. Thus Holden's initial dismissal of family history as "all that David Copperfield kind of crap" suggests his affinity with the traditional American rejection of the kind of bildungsroman which *David Copperfield*, among other Dickens novels, exemplifies. But while Holden fully shares, on the deepest spiritual level, in the isolation of the traditional American hero, nothing enforces our sense of his impotence more than his ineffectual play at orphanhood in an urban wilderness. Enmeshed as he is in a labyrinth of social roles and family expectations, escape—to a sunny cabin near, but not in the woods—is envisaged in terms of a cliché whose eerie precision illuminates the core of desperation that sustains the image. Salinger's hero is wedded to a pattern of thought and aspiration in which he can no longer seriously believe. He invokes it because it is the only form of self-affirmation his culture affords.

If the old dream of regeneration through separation has become both terrifying and foolish, society remains for Holden what it has always been for American heroes—an anti-community which continues to betray its own high birthright for a mess of commercial pottage. Holden's fear of disappearing—an image which joins the beginning and end of the story—as he crosses from one side of the road or street to the other, aptly expresses his sense of the diminishing ground for authenticity in America. The peculiar sense of a materialism so blanketing that it produces a pervasive deadening of affect becomes the mark of the age. One thinks of Sylvia Plath's *The Bell Jar*, whose heroine finds a correlative to the terror of inner emptiness in the social sterility of Madison Avenue glamour—just that world which Holden imagines himself as headed for. Books such as *The Man in the Grey Flannel Suit* and *Sincerely, Willis Wayde*, written to attract a large popular audience, turn these perceptions into the simplified, world-weary clichés of growing up and selling out. But whether cynical or sincere, the protagonists of these novels share with Holden an inability to conceptualize the future as anything but a dead end. "It didn't seem like *any*thing was coming," says Holden, conveying the sense of a world that seems to annihilate the possibility of growth.

Trying to imagine himself a lawyer like his father, Holden wonders if his father knows why he does what he does. Holden knows that lawyers who rake in the cash don't go around saving the innocent. But even if you were such an idealistic fellow, "how would you know if you did it because you really *wanted* to save guys' lives, or because what you really *wanted* to do was be a terrific lawyer, with everybody slapping you on the back and congratulating you in court. . . . " In a society as replete with verbal falsities as this one, how do you trust your own words, your own thoughts? How do you know when you are telling yourself the truth?

Dickens's tales also show adolescence in an urban commercial society to be a dislocating and frightening process. But from *Nicholas Nickleby* through *Great Expectations* there is regularly a kindly, decent figure who provides aid, comfort, and tutelage in time of need. However bad the adult world seems, enough sources of social strength remain to make the protagonist's struggle toward maturity worthwhile. But Holden never finds such an adult. Mr. Spencer, the history teacher who *seems* to take a fatherly interest in him, is actually most interested in shaming and humiliating him. D.B., the older brother he admires, is as emotionally remote from him as is his father, and Holden takes revenge by reviling him for "selling out" to Hollywood. His mother, as he repeatedly notes, is too nervous and anxious herself to do more than pay perfunctory attention to her children's needs. His father is a shadowy abstraction—a corporate lawyer, defined by his preoccupations and vexations. We hear from Phoebe that "Daddy's going to kill you," rather than experience the father directly through any memory of Holden's.

Holden's anxiety, then, is of a specifically contemporary kind. Those adults who should serve as moral tutors and nurturers are neither wholly absent nor fully present. Perhaps, as David Riesman puts it in speaking of middle-class American parents, "they are passing on to him their own contagious, highly diffused anxiety," as they look to others to define values and goals increasingly based upon socially approved ephemera. Yet, however shadowy these adult figures may be, they are as controlling of Holden as is the impersonal, elusive corporate authority which, he knows, ultimately determines the values of his home. Like the corporate structure itself, these adults are profoundly ambiguous figures whose seeming beneficence it is dangerous to trust. All are effectively epitomized in the teacher Mr. Antolini, whose paternal decency may be entwined with a predator's taste for young boys, and whose advice to Holden turns out to be as puzzling, if not as specious, as his midnight hospitality.

Remarking that Holden is a natural student, Mr. Antolini urges education on him for its efficiency: "After a while, you'll have an idea what kind of thoughts your particular size mind should be wearing. For one thing, it may save you an extraordinary amount of time trying on ideas that . . . aren't becoming to you. You'll begin to know your true measurements and dress your mind accordingly." Mr. Antolini's words, like his manners, are glibly seductive, and a trifle coarse. Ideas as garments that one slips on for the fit—a ready-made identity—is a concept not far removed from the kind of stylized performance that Holden detects in the Lunts ("they were *too* good") and Ernie. It is suited to a society that increasingly emphasizes image and appearance as intrinsically valuable; a society in which the mess and pain of a real struggle with ideas and feelings is considered an unwelcome deviation from the approved norm of "personality."

Because Holden's final return to his family, his "going home," is never dramatized, we are deprived of the experience of a reckoning in which some genuine moral insight, in distinction to Mr. Antolini's sartorial version in the quest for knowledge, might occur. Instead, we are left with the sense of a society that Holden can neither accept nor escape. His encounter has only served to increase his sense of himself as a creature at bay. His anxiety is never allayed.

Because Holden is never allowed to imagine or experience himself in any significant struggle with others (his bloody fistfight with Stradlater emphasizes the futility of any gesture that *is* open to him), neither he (nor his creator) can conceive of society as a source of growth, or self-knowledge. In place of a dialectical engagement with others, Holden clings to the kind of inner resistance that keeps exiles and isolates alive. In response to the pressures for "adjustment" which his sanitarium psychiatrists impose, he insists upon the principle that spontaneity and life depend upon "not knowing what you're going to *do* until you do it." If the cost of this shard of freedom is the continuing anxiety which alienation and disaffection bring— of life in a permanent wilderness, so to speak—so be it. Impoverished it may be, but in Holden's sense of "freedom" one can already see foreshadowed the celebrated road imagery of the Beats.

Holden's struggle for a moral purity that the actual corruptions and compromises of American society, or indeed any society, belie is a familiar one to readers of classic American works. But as I have already suggested, for Holden the terms of that struggle are reversed. Unlike nineteenth-century characters, Holden is not an obvious social outsider or outcast to those he lives among. Well-born and well-favored, his appearance, abilities, and manners make him an insider—he belongs. And yet, as the heir of all the ages, blessed with the material splendors of the Promised Land, Holden feels more victim or prisoner than favored son. Like the country at large, he expresses his discomfort, his sense of dis-ease, by squandering his resources— physical, emotional, intellectual—without attempting to utilize them for action and change. But the willfull futility of his acts should not blind us to the psychic truth which they reveal. Ultimately Holden is performing a kind of self-mutilation against that part of himself which is hostage to the society that has shaped him. Moreover, while previous American heroes like Hester

Prynne and Huck Finn evaded social reality at the cost of denying their human need for others and their likeness to them, Holden's resistance concludes on a wistful note of longing for everybody outside the prison of his sanitarium—an ambivalence that aptly fixes the contemporary terms of his predicament.

Holden's self-division is thus reduced to the only form in which his society can bear to consider it—a psychological problem of acceptance and adjustment; yet Salinger's irony results in a curious double focus. The increasing prestige of American psychoanalysis in the 1950s may be attributed to its tendency (at least in the hands of some practicioners) to sever individual issues and conflicts from their connections to more obdurate realities in the social world. There is familiar comfort in the belief that *all* problems are ultimately individual ones which can, at least potentially, be resolved by force of the individual mind and will. This irony surely lies within the compass of Salinger's story. But its effect is undercut by the polarized perspective that Salinger has imposed on his hero. As we have seen, the stoic isolation through which Holden continues to protect his authenticity is itself an ethic that devalues confrontration or action and so fixes human possibility in the mold of a hopeless hope. Indeed, it becomes a strategy for containment, as much an evasion of social reality as is the psychiatric imperative to adjust.

There is nothing finally in Holden's diffuse sympathies to offend or dismay the reader, nothing to keep him permanently on edge. By the end of the story the reader has seen his familiar social world questioned, shaken, only to be reconstituted as an inevitable fate. Having been drawn to Holden's side we are finally drawn to his mode of perception and defense. To keep the citadel of the self intact by keeping others at a distance is the kind of social agreement that guarantees that the longed-for community which American experience forever promises will surely forever be withheld.

In discussing the romantic novelist in nineteenth-century European literature, René Girard remarks that the romantic establishes a Manichean division of self and other, refusing to see how "Self is implicated in Other." But since Gerard's concern is as much with the author as with the characters, he goes on to note that this situation is finally attributable to the novelist who stands behind the character and refuses to free either himself or his character from these limitations. In distinction, a "classic" novelist, such as Cervantes, transcends this opposition by distancing himself from his character and so frees himself from the character's perspective. Some form of reconciliation is then possible between protagonist and world.

In Girard's terms, Salinger never frees himself, or therefore the reader, from the grip of Holden's perspective. What happens is just the reverse. We are initiated into a process of seeing in which we are either on the side of integrity and autonomy (Holden) or on the side of the predators and exploiters—from Maurice the pimp to the anonymous psychoanalyst who wants Holden to promise to "apply" himself. A Manichean choice indeed. For the reader, this duality preempts all other modes of perception. The corrosive materialism that blasts Holden as it does his world finally becomes irrelevant to any particular historical moment or reality. Instead, isolation, anxiety, the modern sickness of soul turns out to be the given, irremediable condition of our lives.

DENNIS McCORT

Hyakujo's Geese, Amban's Doughnuts, and Rilke's Carrousel: Sources East and West for Salinger's Catcher

Zen koans are supra-logical spiritual projects meant to be worked on full-time. Even when the monk is not formally meditating, the koan continues to resonate from the hinterlands of consciousness, suffusing every thought, word and deed with its inpenetrable mystery. So, as Holden Caulfield dutifully attends to the wisdom dispensed to him by his history teacher Mr. Spencer upon his dismissal from Pencey Prep, in the back of his mind an odd question lingers and asserts itself: "I was thinking about the lagoon in Central Park . . . wondering where the ducks went when the lagoon got all icy and frozen over." Holden, of course, knows nothing of Zen, but Salinger wants the *reader* to think of him as working on a koan. The matter of the Central Park ducks, silly though it be on the surface, is to bedevil Holden throughout his lost Christmas weekend in New York City and, like a good koan, will not leave him alone until he comes to terms with the central problem of his life, that is, with his so-called *life* koan, which the ducks symbolize.

Although the topic of Zen in Salinger's writings has often been addressed, coverage has been limited primarily to the fiction collected and published subsequent to *The Catcher in the Rye*—fiction in which the Zen theme is explicit. Among those few commentators who have searched for traces of Zen in *Catcher* in particular, one finds interesting speculation as well

From *Comparative Literature Studies* 34, no. 3 (1997). © 1997 The Pennsylvania State University.

as enlightening discussion of Buddhism in the broad generic sense, but not a single unequivocal reference to the unique Sino-Japanese form of Buddhism known as Zen. This is especially mystifying in the case of Rosen, ninety percent of whose monograph is devoted to the topic. Alsen, perhaps the most authoritative voice on the subject of Salinger's interest in Eastern religion, takes the fictive Buddy Glass' self-characterization as reflective of the author, insisting that Zen is far less important in Salinger's work than "the New and old Testaments, Advaita Vedanta, and classical Taoism."

This is an odd state of affairs. Since Zen figures so prominently in *Nine Stories*, the compositional chronology of which overlaps that of *Catcher*, and so explicitly in the conversational fabric of "Zooey," one would expect to find at least some evidence of it in *Catcher*, the more so since, according to Skow and Lundquist, Salinger had been immersed in Zen studies at least since the mid 1940s. Yet *Catcher* is apparently Zen-less. I propose, by way of explanation, that there are indeed traces of Zen in *Catcher*, at least two traces that are quite subtle, seamlessly woven as they are into character and narrative. They are hence easily overlooked, but nevertheless unequivocal once they are linked to their proper sources in Zen lore. The remainder of this essay purports to establish this linkage and, in so doing, to evoke our appreciation of the way the scenes in question symbolically enrich Holden's characterization. This, in turn, should significantly modify and deepen our understanding of the shifting circumstances of Salinger's interest in Zen.

Symbolic echoes of other literature in the work of a great writer are usually a matter of deliberate encoding. This, however, does not preclude a significant degree of spontaneity from the process, as such echoes often tend, as it were *on their own*, to insinuate themselves in clusters, or even to coalesce in the writer's imagination, much in the way of what Freud called the "overdetermined" or condensed imagery of dreams. Analogous to the dreamer, who has his entire personal history to draw upon in shaping his unconscious narrative, the well-read writer in the throes of creation has a vast "inner library" of texts at his disposal, and the particular focus of that writer's interest in any given moment will tend to draw ("check out") certain of these stored texts to itself metonymically and virtually without effort. As a more or less automatic process, then, literary allusions in texts often freely intermingle, paying no heed to a future interpreter's need for discrete thematic taxonomies or stylistic levels.

Such is the case with Salinger's novel, for it turns out that we cannot fully appreciate the symbolic significance of Zen for Holden Caulfield's final spiritual catharsis without noting its fusion in the penultimate chapter with an allusion to a key image from the work, not of an ancient Chinese or Japanese sage, but of a modern German poet, who, though implicitly Zen-like in many ways, yet most likely had no formal acquaintance with that religion. I refer to none other that Rainer Maria Rilke and his renowned *Dinggedicht*, "Das Karussell." In Salinger's *Catcher in the Rye*, it would seem that sources East and West not only meet but indeed become mutually determining.

HYAKUJO'S GEESE

The first trace of Zen in Salinger's novel takes us back to the above-mentioned ducks, which appear four times in the narrative, in each instance as a seemingly superfluous preoccupation of Holden's. After their introduction as a "quirky mental distraction" during his farewell talk with Mr. Spencer, they recur as a "spontaneous question" put by Holden to the first cabby in chapter nine, then again in conversation with the second cabby in chapter twelve, and finally in chapter twenty as the object of a desperate nocturnal search. Viewed together the four instances form a kind of *leitmotif* structured by a sense of increasing urgency, very much like the build-up of tension that leads to the sudden breakthrough to solution in koan meditation practice.

It is likely this odd blend, of emotional urgency on Holden's part with a seeming irrelevance of the ducks to the narrative in any logical or figurative sense, that initially calls one's attention to them. If the attending reader should happen to be familiar with Zen folklore, he might suddenly recognize the duck's symbolic derivation therein, at which point it would become quite obvious that these "extraneous" fowl lie right at the heart of Holden's identity crisis. Salinger's source for the motif is an antecdote contained in D. T. Suzuki's *Essays in Zen Buddhism (First Series)* which initially appeared in New York in August of 1949 while the author was hard at work on the first draft of *Catcher*. In Essay 5, entitled "On Satori—The Revelation of a New Truth in Zen Buddhism," Suzuki relates the following:

> Hyakujo (Pai-chang Huai-hai, 724–814) one day went out attending his master Baso (Ma-tsu). A flock of wild geese was seen flying and Baso asked:
> "What are they?"
> "They are wild geese, sir."
> "Whither are they flying?"
> "They have flown away, sir."
> Baso, abruptly taking hold of Hyakujo's nose, gave it a twist. Overcome with pain, Hyakujo cried aloud: "Oh! Oh!"

"You say they have flown away," Baso said, "but all the same they have been here from the very beginning."

This made Hyakujo's back wet with cold perspiration. He had satori.

Here the master is testing his student's insight by means of a *mondo*, that is, a sudden question meant to evoke the latter's delusive view on some significant spiritual matter—in this case, the relationship between change and permanence. Hyakujo's conventionally one-sided view of the issue, which sees only change (ducks coming and going), is thrown up to him through Baso's carefully timed nasal shock tactic. The master senses that his mature student needs only a little jolt, some deft act of "compassionate cruelty," to precipitate in him that final *salto mortale* from ignorance to Wisdom. As Hyakujo cries out in pain, the master suddenly calls his attention to the other side of the issue ("all the same they have been here from the very beginning"): change and permanence, the transitory and the abiding, are one and the same, an inseparable identity of opposites. From the Zen point of view, to resolve one contradiction is to resolve them all (since the distinction between the one and the many is itself a delusion). This instantaneous coalescence in his consciousness of all that has heretofore been separate is Hyakujo's satori or Enlightenment. Having propelled the monk from his long-suffering state of separative dualism into the rarified atmosphere of Enlightened monism, Master Baso's *mondo* has served its purpose.

Holden's preoccupation with the ducks is clearly a symbolic extension of this traditional Zen anecdote as recounted in Suzuki's *Essays*. Hyakujo's *mondo* becomes Holden's koan, a koan that embodies the core conflict of his life: how he can hang onto the innocence of childhood while moving, inexorably, into the phony world of adulthood, or, how can he discover that changeless, inviolate innocence that never flies away but "all the same has been here from the very beginning." His brother Allie had found a way to preserve it (as Holden sees it): he died. To the living that is, of course, a one-sided solution: a loved one who died has made himself inaccessible to change in the minds and hearts of the survivors. Such a denouement falls short of the absolutist standards of Zen, in particular of the koan, which demands a solution that somehow includes both terms of the contradiction: both change and permanence, corruption and innocence, in a seamless *coincidentia oppositorum*. In a word, Holden is trying to do the impossible. It will indeed take nothing less than a death to accomplish this, not biological death, but that much more difficult death of the ego, the mystics' "death before death," a conscious and voluntary surrender that is prelude to Enlightenment, the spiritual condition in which all conflicts and contradictions are resolved "suddenly," and forever.

With the ducks' first appearance—in Holden's consciousness during that farewell chat with Mr. Spencer—Salinger makes allusion to an interesting aspect of koan psychology: even when the aspirant allows the koan to move from the center to the periphery of his attention so that he can take up other tasks, the koan continues to exert its influence. Though the monk has stopped working on it, it continues to work on him. Kapleau says of this subliminal dimension of koan work: ". . . once the koan grips the heart and mind . . . the inquiry goes on ceaselessly in the subconscious. While the mind is preoccupied with a particular task, the question fades from consciousness, surfacing naturally as soon as the action is over, not unlike a moving stream which now and again disappears underground only to reappear and resume its open course without interrupting its onward flow." Thus, as Holden tells us:

> The funny thing is, though, I was sort of thinking of something else while I shot the bull [with Mr. Spencer]. . . . I was wondering where the [Central Park] ducks went when the lagoon got all icy and frozen over. I wondered if some guy came in a truck and took them away to a zoo or something. Or if they just flew away.
>
> I'm lucky, though. I mean I could shoot the old bull to old Spencer and think about those ducks at the same time. It's funny. You don't have to think too hard when you talk to a teacher.

Since Holden is only half-listening to Mr. Spencer's sage counsel, the thing that is really on his mind is able to surface in consciousness.

In the three subsequent duck-episodes there is, as noted, a pattern of growing tension as the issue takes on for Holden the tightening grip of an obsession. As one Rinzai master put it in terms of *Mu*, the fundamental Zen koan: "[You must reach the point where you feel] as though you had swallowed a red-hot iron ball that you cannot disgorge despite your every effort." This sense of entrapment by the issue, of feeling utterly unable either to advance or retreat from it, while at the same time compelled to do *something*, is fertile ground for the lightning flash of insight. During his first cab ride through Central Park in chapter nine, Holden puts the question to the surly cabby: "You know those ducks in that lagoon right near Central Park South? That little lake? By any chance, do you happen to know where they go, the ducks, when it gets all frozen over? Do you happen to know, by any chance?" In verbalizing his concern Holden begins to experience the unsettling ubiquity of the koan as it spreads from the private inner to the outer social domain. At the same time he is becoming aware of its frustrating imponderability. For a koan to be effective, the meditator must at some point come up against its diamond-hard resistance to reason, otherwise he will not be driven to arouse his own latent supra-rational resources: "I realized [in asking the cabby] it was only one chance in a million."

Later on, this time in Horwitz's cab, Holden presses the issue further: "Hey, Horwitz. . . . You ever pass by the lagoon in Central Park? . . . Well, you know the ducks that swim around in it? In the springtime and all? Do you happen to know where they go in the wintertime, by any chance?" Unlike his predecessor who dismissed Holden's question with contempt, this cabby engages him in a mock-comic round of what is known in Zen as "dharma duelling," defined by Kapleau as "a verbal joust or battle of 'wit' as respects the dharma, usually between two enlightened persons." Here Horwitz takes the role of Holden's/Hyakujo's enlightened master whose task it is to pry his student loose from a one-sided view of things: whereas Holden continues to brood obsessively on the ephemeral (the vanished ducks, with their unconscious associations to his brother's death and to the impending "death" of his own innocence), Horwitz aggressively calls his attention to the fish frozen in the lagoon which embody constancy:

> "The *fish* don't go no place. They stay right where they are, the fish. Right in the goddam lake."
> "The fish—that's different. The fish is different. I'm talking about the *ducks*," I said.
> "What's *dif*ferent about it? Nothin's *dif*ferent about it," Horwitz said. . . . "Use your head, for Chrissake."

Unlike the mature Hyakujo who teeters on the brink of insight, needing only a sharp tweak of the nose to transcend the logical boundaries of his own mind, Holden stays mired in his "Dark Night," continuing to struggle and resist the master's Truth: "'You don't think them fish just *die* when it gets to be winter, do ya?' 'No, but—.'"

The fourth and final duck-episode, occuring several hours (and drinks) later, finds Holden wandering around Central Park in half-drunken confusion as he presses on with the quest: "I figured I'd go by that little lake and see what the hell the ducks were doing, see if they were around or not." After much fruitless groping and stumbling, "Then, finally, I found it. What it was, it was partly frozen and partly not frozen. But I didn't see any ducks around. I walked all around the whole damn lake—I damn near fell *in* once, in fact—but I didn't see a single duck."

There are in this sequence several allusions to the traditional ordeal of the spiritual path, allusions that are subtle yet unmistakable when viewed in a Zen context. For example, just as the masters warn of sorely testing periods of melancholy, so Holden complains, "I was feeling so damn depressed and lonesome. . . . I wasn't tired or anything. I just felt blue as hell." Also, as one would expect, the motif of darkness is emphasized: "Boy, was it dark. . . . I kept walking and walking, and it kept getting darker and darker and spookier and spookier." Kapleau points out that "In Zen it is said that 'the grand round mirror of wisdom is as black as pitch'" and quotes his teacher Yasutani Roshi's version of St. John's "Dark Night of the Soul": "To renounce such conceptions [i.e., what one presumes to know of the way the world works] is to stand in 'darkness.' Now, satori comes out of this 'darkness,' not out of the 'light' of reason and worldly knowledge."

In its subjective aspect, the darkness motif embodies the anguish of being utterly lost. As another master, Shibayama, has it: "the koan will mercilessly take away all our intellect and knowledge. In short, the role of the koan is not to lead us to satori easily, but on the contrary to make us lose our way and drive us to despair." Thus Holden, even in the park's familiar surroundings: "I had the most terrific trouble finding that lagoon that night. I *knew* right where it was—it was right near Central Park South and all—but I still couldn't find it."

Finally, there is Holden's eventual discovery of the duckless lagoon, "partly frozen and partly not frozen." The qualities of frozenness and fluidity echo Holden's life koan, that is, the painful contradiction between permanence and change, symbolically played out earlier in Holden's duck/fish "dharma duel" with Horwitz. The half-and-half or neither/nor aspect of the lagoon's state alludes to the prickly razor's-edge nature of koan work which prevents the meditator from lapsing into either (or, for that matter, *any*) logical position suggested by the koan. Only the Middle Way, a central tenet of Buddhism, leads by its very a-positional "narrowness" to the promised land of Enlightenment, to the ineffable *coincidentia oppositorum* in which all dualities are transcended, all contradictions resolved. Holden has not yet arrived at the promised land ("But I couldn't find any [ducks]"), but he is, at this point, well along the path.

Although Salinger nowhere mentions Suzuki's *Essays* by name as his source for the ducks, the circumstantial evidence for his having worked with this well-known introductory text during the writing of *Catcher* is compelling. As Hamilton tells us, "From summer 1949 to summer 1950 he seems to have worked flat out on the novel." The British Rider edition of the *Essays in Zen Buddhism* came out in both London and New York in August of 1949. The first American edition of the book appeared in New York City on May 10, 1950, published by HarperCollins (then called "Harper Brothers").

The publication of *Catcher* by Little, Brown and Co. just over a year later, on July 16, 1951, means that Suzuki's book was available to Salinger in its earlier British edition during his writing of the novel's first draft and, in its American edition, during his completion of the draft in spring and summer 1950. This is not to mention the all-important months of revision extending through winter and spring 1951 preceding publication in July.

I say "all-important months of revision" because it was Salinger's working style not simply to revise and edit his stories but virtually to rewrite them again and again, often incorporating in the rewriting, as suggested earlier, new elements culled from various interesting books that came his way. When one considers that Salinger fancied himself a Zen bibliophile, that he makes several references to D. T. Suzuki in the Glass stories, revealing his affinity for this renowned transmitter of Zen culture, and that he can be definitely linked to at least *one* other early 50's book of Suzuki's, it seems virtually certain that a copy of the *Essays* lay not far from the typewriter during his completion of the first draft and revisions of *Catcher*.

AMBAN'S DOUGHNUTS

The second reference in *Catcher* to a specific Zen source occurs only once, in Chapter 25, as Holden walks uptown from Grand Central Station the next morning looking for a place to have breakfast. In the wake of his tearful reunion with Phoebe and traumatic encounter with Mr. Antolini, Holden's spirits have reached their lowest ebb ("I think I was more depressed than I ever was in my whole life"). Beset by morbid hypochondriacal thoughts ("So I figured I was getting cancer"), he thinks he might feel better with something in his stomach:

> So I went in this very cheap-looking restaurant and had doughnuts and coffee. Only, I didn't eat the doughnuts. I couldn't swallow them too well. The thing is, if you get very depressed about something, it's hard as hell to swallow. The waiter was very nice, though. He took them back without charging me. I just drank the coffee.

Holden's gagging on the doughnuts is an allusion to the forty-ninth and final koan contained in the *Mumonkan* (Ch., *Wu-men-kuan: The Gateless Gate*), the renowned medieval Chinese collection assembled in 1228 by Master Mumon Eikai (Wu-men Hui-k'ai). The koan is entitled "Amban's Addition" because a lay student, so-named, later attached it to Mumon's original edition of forty-eight. In it Amban gives a mock portrayal of himself as seeking revenge on old Master Mumon for foisting those forty-eight undigestible koans on any passerby willing to swallow them. The added koan is Amban's "priceless opportunity" to give Mumon a taste of his own medicine:

> Mu-mon has just published forty-eight koans and called the book *Gateless Gate*. He criticizes the old patriarchs' words and actions. I think he is very mischievous. He is like an old doughnut seller trying to catch a passerby to force his doughnuts down his mouth. The customer can neither swallow nor spit out the doughnuts, and this causes suffering. Mu-mon has annoyed everyone enough, so I think I shall add one more as a bargain. I wonder if he himself can eat this bargain. If he can, and digest it well, it will be fine, but if not, we will have to put it back into the frying pan with his forty-eight also and cook them again. Mu-mon, you eat first, before someone else does:
>
> Buddha, according to a sutra, once said: "Stop, stop. Do not speak. The ultimate truth is not even to think."

Undigestible doughnuts are an apt comic image for the psycho-spiritual impasse that koans are designed to produce. Unaided reason does not equip man to comprehend ("swallow") the freedom from, indeed *within*, contradiction (permanence/change, innocence/corruption, childhood/adulthood) promised by Enlightenment. He simply cannot "take it in." Unless he be driven by an intolerable suffocation to summon up from the abyss of consciousness a power equal to this Truth, he will choke on it. Perhaps instinctively sensing this, Holden backs away from the doughnuts before getting completely "stuck." But stuck he is and, at least for a while longer, stuck he will remain between child and grown-up.

Holden's doughnuts echo Amban's doughnuts, and both echo *Mu*, mentioned earlier as the koan of koans or meta-koan. As the signature koan of Rinzai Zen, *Mu* is placed first in the *Mumonkan*. Its wording is as follows:

> A monk asked Joshu [a master], "Has a dog Buddha nature?"
> Joshu answered, "Mu."

This *Mu*, variously "nothing, not, nothingness, un-, is not, has not, not any," is assigned by the *roshi* (master) to most Zen novices as an object of meditation (*zazen*). Like any koan, it is not an intellectual exercise, nor does it have any "correct" answer or interpretation. Any answer, verbal or non-verbal, presented by student to master is correct that demonstrates the former's clear intuitive grasp of the main issue: nothing (no thing) is real, all is emptiness; and hence, by virtue of the *coincidentia oppositorum* portended by the Middle Way of the koan, everything is real, all is fullness. Net result: *Mu* is absolute Freedom, ineffable Mystery, ground zero Truth. Hence its traditional representation in Japanese ink-brush calligraphy as a thick doughnut-shaped cipher. (We noted above *Mu*'s similar characterization by Hakuun Yasutani as a half-swallowed "red-hot iron ball that you cannot disgorge despite your every effort.") Doughnut or iron ball, *Mu* is what nearly chokes Holden.

Salinger's most likely source for the doughnut interlude is Nyogen Senzaki and Paul Reps's 1934 edition of *The Gateless Gate*, published by John Murray in Los Angeles. This likelihood is increased by the compilers' inclusion of Amban's "49th koan," in constrast to its omission by "purist" editors of most other English translations. Salinger is also linked to the Reps by Alsen, who cites another Reps collection, *101 Zen Stories* (1939), as a probable source for the Zen motifs in *Nine Stories* and "Raise High the Roof Beam, Carpenters." The point of emphasis here, of course, is that Salinger was already interpolating specific elements of Zen lore into the creative process as early as *Catcher*.

RILKE'S CARROUSEL AND HOLDEN'S ENLIGHTENMENT

It has been shown that the aim of a koan is, by dint of its logical absurdity, to frustrate the binary either/or structure of ordinary consciousness; in Western terms, to straitjacket the conventional rationalist Aristotelian viewpoint so that something akin to the mystical Platonic can break through. This is why so many koans and anecdotes in the ancient collections feature the imagery of impasse: a monk hanging from a lofty branch by his teeth, or facing the master's bamboo stick no matter what he says or does, or being challenged to take one step forward from atop a 100-foot flagpole. The more oppressive the dilemma, the more favorable the conditions for inner revolution. Clearly the damned-either-way gallows humor of Zen appealed strongly to Salinger's sense of irony. The missing ducks, the half-frozen pond and the gagging doughnuts are intended, as symbolic echoes of classical Zen situations, to lend to an aura of both gravity and, in Balzac's sense, comedy to the situation of a youth mired deep in crisis. The novel is all about Holden's weekend at the crossroads. As the reader approaches the climactic scene at the carrousel, the question verily burns: what will Holden *do*? Similarly, the old Zen masters often put this nakedly terrifying question to their spiritual charges for whom they had just devised some intolerable bind.

What Holden does in fact "do" at the carrousel is resolve his life koan. His subsequent "illness" and therapeutic confinement in no way cast doubt on this. Zen literature is replete with accounts of Enlightenment experiences (*kensho* or *satori*) that are so shattering to the individual's conditioned world view that the rush of emancipation they bring is initially experienced as a kind of nervous breakdown. Kapleau reports the case of one Zen student, a Japanese business executive, who, in his own words, one night

> . . . abruptly awakened. At first my mind was foggy, . . . Then all at once I was struck as though by lightning, and the next instant heaven and earth crumbled and disappeared. Instantaneously, like surging waves, a tremendous delight welled up in me, a veritable hurricane of delight, as I laughed loudly and wildly: "Ha, ha, ha, ha, ha, ha! . . . "
> My son told me later he thought I had gone mad.

What one might call Holden's Divine Madness commences with his sudden announcement of his decision to "go home," made to Phoebe at the carrousel: "'Yeah,' I said. I meant it too. I wasn't lying to her. I really did go home afterwards." Perhaps here too Salinger had in mind Suzuki, who describes Enlightenment in lapsarian-mythical terms as the return of conscious will to its "own original abode where there was yet no dualism, and therefore peace prevailed. This longing for the home, however, cannot be satisfied without a long, hard, trying experience. For the thing [consciousness] once divided in two cannot be restored to its former unity until some struggle is gone through with."

However that may be, there can be little doubt of the Zen reference contained in the rain that then begins to fall, as Holden says, "[i]n *buckets*" (Salinger's emphasis). Holden's cliche is an "inside" Zen allusion to this shattering or explosive quality that often ushers in an Enlightenment experience. The bucket or pail or barrel that has its bottom smashed through, thus releasing the flow of water heretofore "confined," is a traditional Rinzai metaphor for the aspirant's longed-for breakthrough to spiritual freedom. The image may have its origins in the biography of the medieval Japanese master Bassui by his student Myodo who describes the moment of the former's Enlightenment as a feeling of having "lost his life root, like a barrel whose bottom had been smashed open." However, Salinger's source for the image is more likely to have been an anecdote in Senzaki and Reps's *101 Zen Stories* recounting the sudden awakening of the nun Chiyono who "one moonlit night . . . was carrying water in an old pail bound with bamboo. The bamboo broke and the bottom fell out of the pail, and at that moment Chiyono was set free!" Of course, in narrating the climactic event of Holden's spiritual breakthrough, Salinger works some deft displacements on the image to avoid obviousness: the water does not rush out through bottomless buckets, rather it is the buckets (of rain) themselves that come pouring down. Similarly, the analogous onrush of tears expressive of the aspirant's emancipation that usually accompanies the bucket image (Myodo says of Bassui that the tears overflowed, "pouring down his face like rain") is truncated in Holden's case to: "I was damn near bawling, I felt so damn happy, if you want to know the truth."

However, what is truly arresting about Salinger's rendering of *Catcher*'s denouement is the particular way he uses the German poet Rilke's *Dinggedicht*, "Das Karussell" (1908), to say the unsayable, that is, to convey through oblique symbolic allusion the essence of Holden's solution to his life koan. Salinger's veneration of Rilke is well known. Rilke is one of very few poets mentioned by name in the fiction. Also, some preliminary scholarship has been done showing influence, but no one has as yet nearly done justice to the profound connection between Rilke's and Salinger's carrousels.

Both poem and novel are about the loss of innocence marking the passage from childhood to maturity. This, as noted above, is precisely the issue (koan) at the root of Holden's crisis: "How can I possibly move on to a world teeming with phonies [change] without becoming one myself [permanence]?", as it were. The reference to "Das Karussell" as a reflection of the miraculous solution at long last welling up in Holden is contained in the blue coat worn by Phoebe as she rides the carrousel. Giddy with delight, Holden exclaims, "I felt so damn happy, . . . I don't know why. It was just that she looked so damn *nice*, the way she kept going around and around, in her blue coat and all." Blue-clad Phoebe alludes to the "kleines, blaues Mädchen" ["little girl in blue"] who rides the stag in Rilke's lyric and stands for innocence, that is, the child's capacity for complete absorption in the moment of play. In counterpoint, the older girls in "Karussell" riding nearby already have, like Holden, one foot in adulthood and thus are afflicted, as is he, with that relentless self-consciousness that breeds phoniness, the bane of Holden's existence: ". . . Mädchen, helle, diesem Pferdesprunge/fast schon entwachsen; mitten in dem Schwunge/schauen sie auf, irgendwohin, herüber—" [". . . girls, so fair, having all but outgrown such play; in mid-ride they look up, at something, over this way—"]. These girls on Rilke's carrousel, one a child, the others no longer quite, dramatized for Salinger the collision of world views that bedevils Holden.

The solution to any koan is some realization of a dialectical synthesis that shifts the aspirant to a phase of consciousness deeper and more comprehensive than the logico-rational, one that can effortlessly accomodate both terms of the conflict. This realization must be more than intellectual (in fact, intellect need hardly be involved at all); it must have the immediacy of an insight grounded in experience and must take one well beyond the pairs of opposites that are forever dogging the human mind. In Rilke's poem this is subtly indicated in the line, "Und manchesmal ein Lächeln, hergewendet" ["And now and then a wide grin turned this way"]. The wide grin is that of some child on the carrousel; it is "hergewendet" ["turned this way"], that is, toward the poet-persona. Poet and child, for a flickering instant locked in each other's gaze. What else can this be but the realization of the *coincidentia oppositorum*? The poet is the one who is somehow able to grow up while yet remaining a child. As Rilke says elsewhere, in response to an imaginary interlocutor, the poet is gifted with the ability to behold all things, good and bad, genuine and phoney, with the celebratory eyes of a newborn: "Oh sage, Dichter . . . /Woher dein Recht, in jeglichem Kostüme,/in jeder Maske wahr zu sein?/—Ich rühme" ["'So tell me, poet . . . /Wherefore thy right to be in any mask, in any costume true?'/—'I celebrate'"]. Indeed, just like a new-born, the poet beholds things by *becoming* them. As Keats has it: "The poet has no self; he is forever filling some other body." This I take to be Salinger's understanding of Rilke's "Das Karussell," and it is this understanding, rather viscerally than intellectually experienced, that now overcomes Holden like an ancient dream fulfilled, releasing him from his long bondage to a worn-out world view.

To be sure, Holden is no poet in the conventional sense, but I believe Salinger takes "poet" in this deeper archetypal sense shaped by the German-Romantic tradition to which Rilke was heir and which he in fact fulfilled: the poet represents the cutting edge of human spiritual evolution, one who has, at least once, been struck by lightning, one who has made, however tentatively, the quantum leap from human to cosmic consciousness. This notion of the poet also seems to be what Franny is trying to convey to her boyfriend as she struggles to justify her dislike of the self-styled poets in the English Department:

> I mean they're not *real* poets. They're just people that write poems that get published and anthologized all over the place, but they're not *poets*.

The archetype of the poet as (wo)man-child, as a seamless sacerdotal identity of opposites, and therefore as the solution to Holden's koan, is also hinted at in Holden's repeated references at the carrousel to "old Phoebe," the child who incarnates the wisdom of the ages.

In Salinger's multi-veiled allusion to this Rilkean meeting of eyes, this interlocking glance, it is not only man and child, or experience and innocence, that fuse in Holden's at last emancipated spirit, but also, as it were in miniature, the great Wisdom traditions of East and West. For Holden's character, suddenly becoming in this apocalyptic moment more than itself, is a syncretic expression of their mutual recognition of the universal mystical truth of the *coincidentia oppositorum*. In Zen, the recognition of this truth lies at the heart of any koan; in Rilke, its expression reflects a perennial German spiritual insight the lineage of which can be traced back at least as far as Meister Eckhart's "Single Eye" by which man and God view each other. It is Salinger's particular genius in this climactic scene to have brought these great mystical traditions together in the simple, homey tableau of an older brother happily watching his kid sister as she takes a turn on the local merry-go-round. One need hardly point out that all of this is punctuated, so to speak, by the image of the carrousel itself as a mandala-symbol of the dynamic Eye of Wisdom to which the path of Holden Everyyouth inevitably leads.

A final question suggests itself. The Zen masters tell us that to have solved one koan is, at least for a time, to have solved them all, since every koan, upon solution, vouchsafes a glimpse of the "same" Absolute. If, as is argued here, Holden has accomplished this, if, for the duration of his cheerful repose on that park bench (and doubtless well beyond), he basks in the glow of Enlightenment, then why does Salinger have him end his story on a note of lack or deficit, as if he were still ensnared by what Buddhists call *avidya*, that is, the primal Ignorance that gives rise to desire: "About all I know is, I sort of *miss* everybody I told about. Even old Stradlater and Ackley, for instance. I think I even miss that goddam Maurice. It's funny. Don't ever tell anybody anything. If you do, you start missing everybody"?

Oddly, the question answers itself when taken paradoxically, that is, when one reads "missing" in the paradoxical context of Enlightenment, wherein all contradictions are resolved, as *itself* a form, even the supreme form, of "having." C. S. Lewis, no mean adept in spiritual matters, makes this point most eloquently in his autobiographical description of the state of "Joy," i.e., Enlightenment considered in its affective aspect. Recalling his experience of a walk during which this sense of Joy had been especially acute, he reflects

> . . . what I had felt on the walk had also been desire, and only possession in so far as that kind of desire is itself desirable, is the fullest possession we can know on earth; or rather, because the very nature of Joy makes nonsense of our common distinction between having and wanting. There, to have is to want and to want is to have.

For Holden at this moment, to miss is to have—fully. As for his missing "even . . . that goddam Maurice," it is another curious fact of Enlightenment that, viewed through Its eyes, all things assume an aura of infinite value, however noble or base they may rank on the valuative skills of ordinary consciousness. Sizuki goes so far as to say:

> But with the realization of Enlightenment, the whole affair [i.e., life] changes its aspect, and the order instituted by Ignorance is reversed from top to bottom. What was negative is now positive, and what was positive is now negative. Buddhist scholars ought not to forget this revaluation of ideas that comes along with Enlightenment.

To all appearances, Holden Caulfield is neither a poet nor a Buddhist scholar. Yet he is, by novel's end, an intimate of the Truth both stammer to convey.

CONCLUSION

Indications are that Salinger's interest in Zen slowly waned in the course of the 1950's as he turned to other Eastern religions and to Christianity for inspiration. In fact, the gradient of this waning can be traced in terms of the kind of narrative treatment given the Zen motif from *Catcher* (1950) through *Nine Stories* (1953) to "Zooey" (1957) and "Seymour: An Introduction" (1959). Generally speaking, the movement is from implicit to explicit, or from subtext to text. In *Catcher*, Zen has a clear but strictly covert presence. It is there as symbolic echo and oblique allusion, imbuing the "banal" tale of a modern adolescent's identity crisis with the power and gravity of ancient legend. Its use is, in a word, aesthetic—the more so in view of its subtle but profound resonance, as we have seen, with a spiritually akin yet culturally remote literary echo from the German poet Rilke. In *Nine Stories*, Zen still serves a quasi aesthetic function (e.g., Seymour's semi-implicit banana-fish koan, or Teddy's eccentric "emptying-out" theory of education, a transparent reference to the Buddhist concept of *shunyata*), but the one-hand-clapping koan that prefixes the book signals the emergence of Zen as more an intellectual than a creative issue for Salinger. This is precisely its status in "Zooey," where it is lavishly entertained in the probing religious dialogue of brother and sister, and in "Seymour: An Introduction," which features a longish peroration on Zen given by Buddy near its end. As the author's religious enthusiasms shift away from Zen, Zen becomes in the fiction something that has always been anathema to the masters—an object of discussion.

Of course, Salinger is not to be faulted for this. Passions wax and wane, interests come and go, for artists no less than mere mortals. An artist's only duty is to follow his daimon wherever it may lead. The matter of waning interest is raised here only as an attempt to account for the peculiar failure of previous critics to identify specific elements of Zen in *Catcher*. The announced presence of Zen in the later fiction seems to have lulled most of them into the assumption that it has little or no presence in *Catcher*. Ironically, just the opposite is the case: the presence of the East in *Catcher* is all the stronger precisely for its being unnannounced, not to mention covertly commingled with the strains of the poet from the West. Salinger himself recognized this gradual slackening of his ability to make creative use, not only of Zen, but of religion generally, in his work. He fretted over the question whether he really was following his daimon. Hamilton tells us that Salinger, in an unpublished letter to his friend and confidant, Learned Hand, written in the late 1950's, "admits he is well aware that his new [post-Zen] religious preoccupations might turn out to be harmful to his writing, and that he sometimes wishes he could go back to his old methods. But it seemed to him that there was little he could do about controlling the direction of his work." In contrast to Holden who arrives at Enlightenment at the end of a painful inner struggle, Holden's author seems to have been blessed with a touch of Enlightenment at the beginning, only to have it calcify with the passing years into something not unlike those glass-encased exhibits in his masterly novel.

STEPHEN J. WHITFIELD

Cherished and Cursed: Toward a Social History of The Catcher in the Rye

The plot is brief: in 1949 or perhaps 1950, over the course of three days during the Christmas season, a sixteen-year-old takes a picaresque journey to his New York City home from the third private school to expel him. The narrator recounts his experiences and opinions from a sanitarium in California. A heavy smoker, Holden Caulfield claims to be already six feet, two inches tall and to have wisps of grey hair; and he wonders what happens to the ducks when the ponds freeze in winter. The novel was published on 16 July 1951, sold for $3.00, and was a Book-of-the-Month Club selection. Within two weeks, it had been reprinted five times, the next month three more times—though by the third edition the jacket photograph of the author had quietly disappeared. His book stayed on the best-seller list for thirty weeks, though never above fourth place.

Costing 75¢, the Bantam paperback edition appeared in 1964. By 1981, when the same edition went for $2.50, sales still held steady, between twenty and thirty thousand copies per month, about a quarter of a million copies annually. In paperback the novel sold over three million copies between 1953 and 1964, climbed even higher by the 1980s, and continues to attract about as many buyers as it did in 1951. The durability of its appeal is astonishing. *The Catcher in the Rye* has gone through over seventy printings and has spread into thirty languages. Three decades after it first

From *New England Quarterly* 70, no. 4 (December 1997). © 1997 *The New England Quarterly*.

appeared, a mint copy of the first edition was already fetching about $200.

Critical and academic interest has been less consistent; and how J. D. Salinger's only novel achieved acclaim is still a bit mystifying. After its first impact came neglect: following the book reviews, only three critical pieces appeared in the first five years. In the next four years, at least seventy essays on *The Catcher in the Rye* were published in American and British magazines. Salinger's biographer explained why: "A feature of the youthquake was, of course, that students could now tell their teachers what to read." Ian Hamilton also notes that by the mid-1950s the novel had "become the book all brooding adolescents had to buy, [and on campuses] the indispensable manual from which cool styles of disaffection could be borrowed." No American writer over the past half-century has entranced serious young readers more than Salinger, whose novel about the flight from Pencey Prep may lag behind only *Of Mice and Men* on public-school required reading lists. And his fiction has inspired other writers as well; the late Harold Brodkey, for example, considered it "the most influential body of work in English prose by anyone since Hemingway."

One explanation for why *The Catcher in the Rye* has enjoyed such a sustained readership came over two decades after the novel was first published—from a middle-aged Holden Caulfield himself, as imagined by journalist Stefan Kanfer: "The new audience is never very different from the old Holden. They may not know the words, but they can hum along with the malady. My distress is theirs. They, too, long for the role of adolescent savior. They, too, are aware of the imminent death in life. As far as the sexual explosion is concerned, I suspect a lot of what you've heard is just noise." Sex "still remains a mystery to the adolescent. I have no cure, only consolation: someone has passed this way before." Objections to schlock and vulgarity and physical decline, and preferences for the pastoral over the machine continue to resonate, "Holden" suspects; and so long as the United States continues to operate very much this side of paradise, a reluctance to inherit what the grown-ups have bequeathed is bound to enlist sympathy. The fantasy of withdrawal and retreat to the countryside ("Massachusetts and Vermont, and all around there . . . [are] beautiful as hell up there. It really is.") is not only a commonplace yearning but also advice Holden's creator elected to take by moving to Cornish, New Hampshire.

But it should be conceded that generally it's the grown-ups who are in charge, and many of them have wanted to ban the widely beloved novel. Why *The Catcher in the Rye* has been censored (and censured) as well as cherished is a curiosity worth examining for its own sake. But how so transparently charming a novel can also exercise a peculiar allure and even emit disturbing danger signals may serve as an entrée into postwar American culture as well.

BAD BOYS, BAD READERS

One weird episode inspired by *The Catcher in the Rye* involves Jerry Lewis. He tried to buy the movie rights, which were not for sale, and to play the lead. One problem was that the director did not read the book until the 1960s, when he was well into his thirties. Playing the protagonist would have been a stretch, but *le roi de crazy* felt some affinity for Salinger (whom Lewis never met): "He's nuts also." Curiously Holden himself mentions the word "crazy" and its cognates (like "mad," "madman," and "insane") over fifty times, more than the reverberant "phony."

Indeed the history of this novel cannot be disentangled from the way the mentally unbalanced have read it. In one instance the reader is himself fictional: the protagonist of John Fowles's first book, which captures the unnerving character of Salinger's only novel as an index of taste, perhaps of moral taste. In the second section of *The Collector*, told from the viewpoint of the victim, the kidnapped Miranda Grey recounts in her diary that she asks her captor, lepidopterist Frederick Clegg, whether he reads "proper books— real books." When he admits that "light novels are more my line," she recommends *The Catcher in the Rye* instead: "I've almost finished it. Do you know I've read it twice and I'm five years younger than you are?" Sullenly he promises to read it. Later she notices him doing so, "several times . . . look[ing] to see how many pages more he had to read. He reads it only to show me how hard he is trying." After the duty has been discharged, over a week later, the collector admits: "I don't see much point in it." When Miranda counters, "You realize this is one of the most brilliant studies of adolescence ever written?" he responds that Holden "sounds a mess to me."

> "Of course he's a mess. But he realizes he's a mess, he tries to express what he feels, he's a human being for all his faults. Don't you even feel sorry for him?"
>
> "I don't like the way he talks."
>
> "I don't like the way you talk," she replies. "But I don't treat you as below any serious notice or sympathy."
>
> Clegg acknowledges: "I suppose it's very clever. To write like that and all."
>
> "I gave you that book to read because I thought you would feel identified with him. You're a Holden Caulfield. He doesn't fit anywhere and you don't."
>
> "I don't wonder, the way he goes on. He doesn't try to fit."
>
> Miranda insists: "He tries to construct some sort of reality in his life, some sort of decency."

"It's not realistic. Going to a posh school and his parents having money. He wouldn't behave like that. In my opinion."

She has the final word (at least in her diary): "You get on the back of everything vital, everything trying to be honest and free, and you bear it down."

Modern art, she realizes, embarrasses and fascinates Clegg; it "shocks him" and stirs "guilty ideas in him" because he sees it as "*all* vaguely immoral." For the mass audience at which William Wyler's 1965 film adaptation was aimed, Clegg's aesthetic world is made less repellent and more conventional, and the conversation about *The Catcher in the Rye* is abbreviated.

In a more class-conscious society than is the United States, Fowles's loner finds something repugnant about the recklessness of the privileged protagonist. In a more violent society than England, types like Frederick Clegg might identify with Holden Caulfield's alienation from "normal" people so thoroughly that they become assassins. To be sure, *The Catcher in the Rye* is bereft of violence; and no novel seems less likely to activate the impulse to "lock and load." But this book nevertheless has exercised an eerie allure for asocial young men who, glomming on to Holden's estrangement, yield to the terrifying temptations of murder. "Lacking a sense of who he is," such a person "shops among artifacts of our culture—books, movies, TV programs, song lyrics, newspaper clippings—to fashion a character." Instead of authentic individuality, Priscilla Johnson McMillan has written, "all that is left is a collection of cultural shards—the bits and pieces of popular culture, torn from their contexts."

In December 1980, with a copy of Salinger's novel in his pocket, Mark David Chapman murdered John Lennon. Before the police arrived, the assassin began reading the novel to himself and, when he was sentenced, read aloud the passage that begins with "anyway, I keep picturing all these little kids" and ends with "I'd just be the catcher in the rye and all." Daniel M. Stashower has speculated ingeniously that Chapman wanted the former Beatle's innocence to be preserved in the only way possible—by death (the fate of Holden's revered brother Allie). Of course it could be argued that the assassin was not a conscientious reader, since Holden realizes on the carrousel that children have to be left alone, that they cannot be saved from themselves: "The thing with kids is, if they want to grab for the gold ring, you have to let them do it, and not say anything. If they fall off, they fall off." No older catcher should try to intervene.

Nor was Chapman the only Beatles fan to reify happiness as a warm gun. John Hinckley, Jr., described himself in his high school days as "a rebel without a cause" and was shocked to hear that Lennon had been murdered.

A year later Hinckley himself tried to kill President Reagan. In Hinckley's hotel room, police found, along with a 1981 John Lennon color calendar, Salinger's novel among a half-dozen paperbacks. Noting the "gruesome congruences between these loners," Richard Schickel wondered whether Chapman and Hinckley could "really believe their disaffections were similar to Holden Caulfield's."

One stab at an answer would be provided in John Guare's play *Six Degrees of Separation*, which opened in New York in 1990 and which he adapted for Fred Schepsi's film three years later. An imposter calling himself Paul insinuates himself into a well-heeled family; he is a perfect stranger (or appears to be). Pretending to be a Harvard undergraduate who has just been mugged, posing as the son of actor Sidney Poitier, Paul claims that his thesis is devoted to Salinger's novel and its odd connections to criminal loners:

> A substitute teacher out on Long Island was dropped from his job for fighting with a student. A few weeks later, the teacher returned to the classroom, shot the student unsuccessfully, held the class hostage and then shot himself. Successfully. This fact caught my eye: last sentence. *Times.* A neighbor described him as a nice boy. Always reading *Catcher in the Rye.*

Paul then mentions "the nitwit—Chapman" and insists that "the reading of that book would be his defense" for having killed Lennon. Hinckley, too, had "said if you want my defense all you have to do is read *Catcher in the Rye.* It seemed to be time to read it again." Paul reads it as a "manifesto of hate" against phonies,

> a touching story, comic because the boy wants to do so much and can't do anything. Hates all phoniness and only lies to others. Wants everyone to like him, is only hateful, and is completely self-involved. In other words, a pretty accurate picture of a male adolescent. And what alarms me about the book—not the book so much as the aura about it—is this: The book is primarily about paralysis. The boy can't function. And at the end, before he can run away and start a new life, it starts to rain and he folds. . . . But the aura around this book of Salinger's—which perhaps should be read by everyone *but* young men—is this: It mirrors like a fun house mirror and amplifies like a distorted speaker one of the great tragedies of

our times—the death of the imagination, [which] now stands as
a synonym for something outside ourselves.

A smooth liar, Paul later admits (or claims) that a Groton commencement
address delivered a couple of years earlier was the source of his insights.

BELOVED AND BANNED

Holden has thus been born to trouble—yet another reminder that, in the
opinion of long queues of literary critics, you can't know anything about him
without your having read a book by Mr. Mark Twain called *The Adventures of
Huckleberry Finn*, which told the truth mainly about the intensity of the
yearning for authenticity and innocence that marks the picaresque quest.
Huck and Holden share the fate of being both beloved *and* banned; such
reactions were not unrelated. When the Concord (Massachusetts) public
library proscribed *The Adventures of Huckleberry Finn* soon after its
publication, the author gloated that not even his *Innocents Abroad* had sold
more copies more quickly; and "those idiots in Concord" "have given us a
rattling tip-top puff which will go into every paper in the country. . . . That
will sell 25,000 copies for us sure."

Salinger's novel does not appear to have been kept off the shelves in
Concord but did cause enough of a stir to make the short list of the most
banned books in school libraries, curricula, and public libraries. In 1973 the
American School Board Journal called this monster best-seller "the most widely
censored book in the United States." It was noted nearly a decade later that
The Catcher in the Rye "had the dubious distinction of being at once the most
frequently censored book across the nation and the second-most frequently
taught novel in public high schools." Anne Levinson, the assistant director of
the Office of Intellectual Freedom in Chicago, called *The Catcher in the Rye*
probably "a perennial No. 1 on the censorship hit list," narrowly ahead of *Of
Mice and Men* and *The Grapes of Wrath* and perhaps Eldridge Cleaver's *Soul
on Ice* as well. No postwar American novel has been subjected to more—and
more intense—efforts to prevent the young from reading it.

Some examples: The National Organization for Decent Literature
declared it objectionable by 1956. Five years later a teacher in a San Jose,
California, high school who had included the novel on the twelfth-grade
supplementary reading list was transferred and the novel dropped. *The
Catcher in the Rye* was excised from the list of approved books in Kershaw
County, South Carolina, after the sheriff of Camden declared part of the
novel obscene. In 1978 the novel was banned in the high schools of Issaquah,
Washington, in the wake of a campaign led by a diligent citizen who

tabulated 785 "profanities" and charged that including Holden in the syllabus was "part of an overall Communist plot in which a lot of people are used and may not even be aware of it." Three school board members in Issaquah not only voted in favor of banning *The Catcher in the Rye* but also against renewing the contract of the school superintendent who had explicitly sanctioned the right of English teachers to assign the book. The board members were recalled, however. A school board member also confiscated a copy of Salinger's novel from a high school library in Asheville, North Carolina, in 1973. Several high school teachers have been fired or forced to resign for having assigned *The Catcher in the Rye*.

California was the site of two well-reported incidents. The first erupted in 1962 in Temple City, near Pasadena, at a Board of Education meeting. Salinger's book had been assigned as supplementary reading for the eleventh grade. A parent objected, in the main, to the "crude, profane and obscene" language. For good measure, though, the book was also condemned for its literary assault on patriotism, "home life, [the] teaching profession, religion and so forth." Another vigilant parent, imploring the President of the United States summarily to fire anyone writing such a book, had obviously confused the reclusive novelist with John F. Kennedy's amiable press secretary, Pierre Salinger.

The Catcher in the Rye was also banned from the supplementary reading list of Boron High School, located on the edge of the Mojave Desert. The proscription had an interesting effect. Salinger "has gained a new readership among townspeople," the *New York Times* reported, "and Helen Nelson, the local librarian, has a waiting list of fifteen people for the book that she says has been sitting on the shelf all these years pretty much unnoticed." The campaign against the book had been fueled by its profanity, which aroused the most heated objections. Vickie Swindler, the parent of a fourteen-year-old girl, was startled to see three "goddamns" on page 32. She recalled phoning the school and demanding to know: "How the hell [*sic*] did this teacher [Shelley Keller-Gage] get this book?" Locals who sympathized with the censors offered a curious interpretation of their motives, which they compared to Holden's dream of becoming a catcher in the rye to keep innocence intact; the protagonist and the parents trying to muzzle him shared a desire to exempt children from the vulgarity and corruption of the adult world. Yet, as Mrs. Keller-Gage noted, "Things are not innocent any more, and I think we've got to help them [i.e., children] deal with that, to make responsible choices, to be responsible citizens." Parents were "wanting to preserve the innocence of the children" in vain. The *Times* reported that she offered an alternative assignment for pupils whose parents were opposed to *The Catcher in the Rye*: Ray Bradbury's *Dandelion Wine*.

When the ban took effect in the new term, Mrs. Keller-Gage put her three dozen copies of Salinger's novel "on a top shelf of her classroom closet, inside a tightly taped cardboard box." Raise high the bookshelf, censors. In place of *The Catcher in the Rye*, she announced, she would assign another Bradbury novel, *Fahrenheit 451*, the title referring to the presumed "temperature at which book-paper catches fire, and burns." This dystopian novel about book-burning was published in 1953, though a shorter version, entitled "The Fireman," had appeared in *Galaxy Science Fiction* in 1950. Both versions were too early to allude to Salinger's novel, which is neither shown nor recited in François Truffaut's 1966 film adaptation (though one item visibly consumed is an issue of *Cahiers du Cinéma*).

Efforts at suppression were not confined to secondary schools. A prominent Houston attorney, "whose daughter had been assigned the novel in an English class at the University of Texas, threatened to remove the girl from the University," *Harper's* reported. "The aggrieved father sent copies [of the novel] to the governor, the chancellor of the university, and a number of state officials. The state senator from Houston threatened to read passages from the book on the senate floor to show the sort of thing they teach in Austin. The lawyer-father said Salinger used language 'no sane person would use' and accused the university of 'corrupting the moral fibers [*sic*] of our youth." He conceded that the novel "is not a hard-core Communist-type book, but it encourages a lessening of spiritual values which in turn leads to communism."

In making appointments to the department of English at the University of Montana, Leslie A. Fiedler recalled that "the only unforgivable thing in the university or the state was to be 'controversial.'" He nevertheless "began to make offers to young instructors who had quarreled with their administrators, or had asked their students to read *Catcher in the Rye*, or had themselves written poetry containing dirty words, or were flagrantly Jewish or simply Black." The narrator of a recent academic novel, *Mustang Sally*, recalls that "the chairman of the department has asked us all to use our best judgment in avoiding confrontation with the evangelicals . . . such as the group who staged a 'pray-in' at the Greensburg High School library because *The Catcher in the Rye* was on the shelves. It has since been removed, along with the principal." No wonder, then, that one columnist, though writing for the newspaper of record, whimsically claimed to "lose count of the number of times the book has been challenged or banned."

Such animosity had become a predictable feature of the far right by the 1980s, when an outfit named Educational Research Analysts, financed by Richard Viguerie, a leading fundraiser for right-wing organizations, was formed to examine nearly every textbook considered for adoption anywhere in the nation. "The group has assembled a list of 67 categories under which a book may be banned. Category 43 ('Trash') included *The Catcher in the Rye*," the *New Republic* reported. Perhaps Salinger should have counted his blessings, since the eclectic Category 44 consisted of the "works of questionable writers" like Malcolm X, Langston Hughes, and Ogden Nash.

It is more surprising that moral objections surfaced in the pages of *Ramparts*, the brashest of the magazines to give a radical tincture to the 1960s. The monthly had begun under Roman Catholic auspices, however; and though Simone de Beauvoir's *The Second Sex* was deemed a work of depravity on the *Index Librorum Prohibitorum*, Salinger was accorded the same treatment as Genet, Proust, Joyce, and D. H. Lawrence: omission. But individual Catholics could still get incensed over *The Catcher in the Rye*, as the new editor of *Ramparts*, Warren Hinckle, discovered one evening. He was having a conversation with the new fiction editor, Helen Keating, who was married to the magazine's new publisher. Hinckle recalled:

> A great debate somehow began over the rather precious subject of J. D. Salinger. The setting was vaguely Inquisitional. . . . They all listened attentively as [Edward] Keating, suddenly a fiery prosecutor, denounced Salinger for moral turpitude. Keating expressed similar opinions about the degeneracy of writers such as Tennessee Williams and Henry Miller: corruption, moral decay, the erosion of the classic values of Western Civilization, et cetera, ad infinitum. His special contempt for Salinger seemed to have something to do with the fact that he had found his oldest son reading a paperback book by the man.

Keating became enraged enough to make "the hyperbolic assertion, which he later retracted, that if he were President, he would put J. D. Salinger in jail! I asked why. 'Because he's dirty,' Ed said. I barely recalled something in *The Catcher in the Rye* about Holden Caulfield in the back seat unhooking a girl's bra," Hinckle recalled. Despite the lyric, "If a body catch a body," in fact few popular novels are so fully exempt from the leer of the sensualist; and even though Holden claims to be "probably the biggest sex maniac you ever saw," he admits it's only "in my *mind*."

In any case, Hinckle was baffled by Keating's tirade and "unleashed a more impassioned defense of Salinger than I normally would have felt impelled to make of a voguish writer whose mortal sin was his Ivy League slickness." The chief consequence of the argument was Keating's discovery of a "bomb," by which he meant "a hot story. The 'bomb' which exploded in the first issue of *Ramparts* was the idea of a symposium on J. D. Salinger"— with Hinckle for the defense and Keating and a friend of his for the prosecution. That friend, Robert O. Bowen, complained in the inaugural issue in 1962 that Salinger was not only anti-Catholic but somehow also "pro-Jewish and pro-Negro." Bowen accused the novelist of being so subversive that he was "vehemently anti-Army" (though Salinger had landed on Utah Beach on D-Day), "even anti-America," a writer who subscribed to "the sick line transmitted by Mort Sahl" and other "cosmopolitan think people." Though Bowen was vague in identifying the sinister campaigns this impenetrably private novelist was managing to wage, alignments with the Anti-Defamation League and "other Jewish pressure groups" were duly noted, and Salinger's sympathy for "Negro chauvinism" was denounced. "Let those of us who are Christian and who love life lay this book aside as the weapon of an enemy," Bowen advised. Such was the level of literary analysis at the birth of *Ramparts*.

The *Catcher in the Rye* has even taken on an iconic significance precisely because it is reviled as well as revered. What if the Third Reich had won the Second World War by defeating Britain? one novelist has wondered. Set in 1964, *Fatherland* imagines a past in which Salinger is among four foreign authors listed as objectionable to the Greater Reich. Those writers, banned by the authorities, are esteemed by younger Germans "rebelling against their parents. Questioning the state. Listening to American radio stations. Circulating their crudely printed copies of proscribed books. . . . Chiefly, they protested against the war—the seemingly endless struggle against the American-backed Soviet guerrillas." But forget about a history that never happened. One of the two regimes that *had* supplanted the defeated Reich was the German Democratic Republic, whose censors were wary of American cultural imports. In the 1960s, Kurt Hager served as the leading ideologist on the Central Committee of the East German regime. Resisting publication of a translation of Salinger's novel, Hager feared that its protagonist might captivate Communist youth. Though a translation did eventually appear and proved popular among young readers in the GDR, Hager refused to give up the fight. Appropriate role models were "winners," he insisted, like the regime's Olympic athletes, not "losers" like Holden Caulfield.

Yet anti-anti-Communism could make use of the novel too. Its reputation for inciting censorious anxiety had become so great by 1990 that in the film *Guilty by Suspicion*, a terrified screenwriter is shown burning his books in his driveway a few hours after testifying before a rump session of the House Un-American Activities Committee. Shocked at this bonfire of the humanities, director David Merrill (Robert De Niro) categorizes what goes up in flames as "all good books"—though the only titles he cites are *The Adventures of Tom Sawyer* and *The Catcher in the Rye*. The decision of writer-director Irwin Winkler to include Salinger's novel, however, is historically (if not canonically) implausible. When the film opens in September 1951, Merrill is shown returning from two months in France; a hot-off-the-press copy of the best-seller must therefore have been rushed to him in Paris if he could pronounce on the merits of the book on his first evening back in Los Angeles.

The attacks on *The Catcher in the Rye* gathered a momentum of their own and "show no signs of tapering off," one student of book-banning concluded in 1979. The novel became so notorious for igniting controversy "that many censors freely admit they have never read it, but are relying on the reputation the book has garnered." Anne Levinson added: "Usually the complaints have to do with blasphemy or what people feel is irreligious. Or they say they find the language generally offensive or vulgar, or there is a sort of general 'family values' kind of complaint, that the book undermines parental authority, that the portrayal of Holden Caulfield is not a good role model for teenagers." It was judged suitable for Chelsea Clinton, however. In 1993 the First Lady gave her daughter a copy to read while vacationing on Martha's Vineyard. The *Boston Globe* used the occasion to editorialize against persistent censorship, since "Salinger's novel of a 1950s coming of age still ranks among the works most frequently challenged by parents seeking to sanitize their children's school reading."

ASSIGNING MEANING TO GROWING UP ABSURD

Few American novels of the postwar era have elicited as much scholarly and critical attention as *The Catcher in the Rye*, and therefore little that is fresh can still be proposed about so closely analyzed a text. But the social context within which the novel has generated such anxiety remains open to interpretation. If anything new can be said about this book, its status within the cross-hairs of censors offers the greatest promise. What needs further consideration is not why this novel is so endearing but why it has inspired campaigns to ban it. Literary critics have tended to expose the uncanny artistry by which Salinger made Holden Caulfield into the loved one but have been far less curious about the intensity of the desire to muffle him. It is nevertheless possible to isolate several explanations for the power of this novel to affect—and disturb—readers outside of departments of English.

The "culture wars" of the last third of the twentieth century are fundamentally debates about the 1960s. The decade marked the end of what historian Tom Engelhardt has labeled "victory culture," indeed the end of "the American Way of Life," phrased in the singular. The 1960s constituted a cæsura in the formation of national self-definition, nor has confidence in *e pluribus unum* been entirely restored. At first glance it might seem surprising for *The Catcher in the Rye* to have contributed in some small fashion to fragmentation. Nevertheless such a case, however tentative, has been advanced. Since nothing in history is created *ex nihilo*, at least part of the 1960s, it has been argued, must have sprung from at least part of the 1950s.

Literary critics Carol and Richard Ohmann, for example, concede that the young narrator lacks the will to try to change society. They nevertheless contend that his creator recorded "a serious critical mimesis of bourgeois life in the Eastern United States, ca. 1950—of snobbery, privilege, class injury, culture as a badge of superiority, sexual exploitation, education subordinated to status, warped social feeling, competitiveness, stunted human possibility, the list could go on." They praise Salinger's acuity "in imagining these hurtful things, though not in explaining them"—or in hinting how they might be corrected. *The Catcher in the Rye* thus "mirrors a contradiction of bourgeois society" and of "advanced capitalism," which promises many good things but frustrates their acquisition and equitable distribution. In this manner readers are encouraged at least to conceive of the urgent *need* for change, even if they're not able to reconfigure Holden's musings into a manual for enacting it.

That moment would have to await the crisis of the Vietnam War, which "converted Salinger's novel into a catalyst for revolt, converting anomie into objectified anger," John Seelye has argued. *The Catcher in the Rye* became "a threshold text to the decade of the sixties, ten years after it appeared at the start of the fifties, [when it was] a minority text stating a minor view." In the axial shift to the left that occurred in the 1960s, the sensibility of a prep school drop-out could be re-charged and politicized: "*Catcher* likewise supplied not only the rationale for the antiwar, anti-regimentation movements of the sixties and seventies but provided the anti-ideological basis for many of the actual novels about Vietnam."

The 1960s mavericks ("the highly sensitive, the tormented") who would brand social injustice as itself obscene were, according to Charles Reich, real-life versions of what Holden had groped toward becoming. Salinger's protagonist may be too young, or too rich, to bestir himself outward. But he was "a fictional version of the first young precursors of Consciousness III. Perhaps there was always a bit of Consciousness III in every teenager, but normally it quickly vanished. Holden sees through the established world: they are phonies and he is merciless in his honesty. But what was someone like Holden to do? A subculture of 'beats' grew up, and a beatnik world flourished briefly, but for most people it represented only another dead end," Reich commented. "Other Holdens might reject the legal profession and might try teaching literature or writing instead, letting their hair grow a little bit longer as well. But they remained separated individuals, usually ones from affluent but unhappy, tortured family backgrounds, and their differences with society were paid for by isolation." In making America more green, Holden was portrayed as an avatar of "subterranean awareness."

Daniel Isaacson also reads the novel as seeding later revolt. The narrator of E. L. Doctorow's *The Book of Daniel*, published exactly two decades after *The Catcher in the Rye*, even echoes Holden in self-consciously repudiating Dickens's contribution to Con II: "Let's see, what other David Copperfield kind of crap" should he tell you? But the personal quickly becomes political, when Daniel insists that "the Trustees of Ohio State were right in 1956 when they canned the English instructor for assigning *Catcher in the Rye* to his freshman class. They knew there is no qualitative difference between the kid who thinks it's funny to fart in chapel, and Che Guevara. They knew then Holden Caulfield would found SDS."

Of course Daniel thinks of himself as an outcast and is eager to re-establish and legitimate his radical lineage, and so his assumption that the trustees might have been shrewd enough to foresee guerrillas in the mist must be treated with skepticism. But consider Tom Hayden, a founder of Students for a Democratic Society (and in the 1950s a parishioner of Father Charles Coughlin in Royal Oak, Michigan). As a teenager Hayden had considered Salinger's protagonist (along with novelist Jack Kerouac and actor James Dean) an "alternative cultural model." "The life crises they personified spawned . . . political activism," which some who had been adolescents in the 1950s found liberating. Hayden remembers being touched not only by Holden's assault on the "phonies" and conformists but by his "caring side," his sympathy for "underdogs and innocents." The very "attempt to be gentle and humane . . . makes Holden a loser in the 'game' of life. Unable to be the kind of man required by prep schools and corporations," Salinger's protagonist could find no exit within American society. Undefiant and confused, Holden nevertheless served as "the first image of middle-class youth growing up absurd," which Hayden would situate at the psychological center of the Port Huron Statement.

The dynamism inherent in youthful revolt, one historian has claimed, can best be defined as "a mystique . . . that fused elements of Marlon Brando's role in *The Wild One*, James Dean's portrayal in *Rebel without a Cause*, J. D. Salinger's Holden Caulfield in *Catcher in the Rye*, the rebels of *Blackboard Jungle*, and the driving energy and aggressive sexuality of the new heroes of rock 'n' roll into a single image. The mystique emphasized a hunger for authenticity and sensitivity." But something is askew here, for Holden is too young to have felt the Dionysian effects of rock 'n' roll, which erupted about three years after he left Pencey Prep. A "sex maniac" only in his head, he hardly represents "aggressive sexuality" either. *The Wild One*, *Rebel without a Cause*, and *Blackboard Jungle* are "goddam movies," which Holden professes to hate, because "they can ruin you. I'm not kidding." His own tastes are emphatically literary, ranging from *The Great Gatsby* and *Out of Africa* to Thomas Hardy and Ring Lardner. Even if the bland official ethos of the 1950s ultimately failed to repress the rambunctious energies the popular arts were about to unleash, Roland Marchand understands that the "mystique" he has identified would not be easily radicalized. Indeed, it could be tamed. Conservative consolidation was a more predictable outcome: "If the problems of a society are embedded in its social structure and are insulated from change by layers of ideological tradition, popular culture is an unlikely source of remedy. It is far more likely to serve needs for diversion and transitory compensation . . . [and] solace." Such dynamism could not be politicized.

The deeper flaw with interpreting *The Catcher in the Rye* as a harbinger of revolt is the aura of passivity that pervades the novel. Alienation does not always lead to, and can remain the antonym of, action. Salinger's own sensibility was definitively pre- (or anti-) Sixties. His "conviction that our inner lives greatly matter," John Updike observed in 1961, "peculiarly qualifies him to sing of an America, where, for most of us, there seems little to do but to feel. Introversion, perhaps, has been forced upon history" rather than the other way around. Therefore "an age of nuance, of ambiguous gestures and pyschological jockeying" could account for the popularity of Salinger's work.

Describing Holden as "a misfit in society because he refuses to adjust" and because he lacks the self-discipline to cultivate privacy, one young literary critic of the fifties was struck by "the quixotic futility" of the protagonist's "outrage" at all the planet's obscenities, by his isolation. Holden seems to have sat for psychologist Kenneth Keniston's portrait of uncommitted youth: those who have the most to live for but find no one to look up to; those who are the most economically and socially advantaged but feel the deepest pangs of alienation. Jack Newfield ('60) was a charter member of SDS but remembers Hunter College as mired in an apathy "no public question seemed to touch." His fellow students "were bereft of passions, of dreams, of gods. . . . And their *Zeitgeist*—J. D. Salinger—stood for a total withdrawal from reality into the womb of childhood, innocence, and mystical Zen." Holden's creator, evidently, had captured the spirit of the Silent Generation.

It may not be accidental that David Riesman, whose most famous book was a veritable touchstone of social analysis in the era, assigned *The Catcher in the Rye* in his Harvard sociology course on Character and Social Structure in the United States. He did so "perhaps," a *Time* reporter speculated, "because every campus has its lonely crowd of imitation Holdens." Indeed, Holden demonstrates the characteristics of anomie, which is associated with "ruleless" and "ungoverned" conduct, that Riesman had described in *The Lonely Crowd;* the anomic are "virtually synonymous with [the] maladjusted." Though Salinger's narrator does not quite exhibit "the lack of emotion and emptiness of expression" by which "the ambulatory patients of modern culture" can be recognized, he does display a "vehement hatred of institutional confines" that was bound to make his peers (if not his psychoanalyst) uneasy. One reviewer, in true Fifties fashion, even blamed Holden himself for his loneliness, "because he has shut himself away from the normal activities of boyhood, games, the outdoors, friendship." It is true that Holden hates schools like Pencey Prep, where "you have to keep making believe you give a damn if the football team loses, and all you do is talk about girls and liquor and sex all day, and everybody sticks together in these dirty little goddam cliques." But Holden remains confined to his era, unable to connect the dots from those cliques to a larger society that might merit some rearrangement. Nor does the novel expand the reader's horizons beyond those of the narrator; it does not get from pathos to indignation.

For *The Catcher in the Rye* is utterly apolitical—unlike its only rival in arousing the ire of conservative parents. Steinbeck's fiction directs the attention of susceptible young readers to exploitation of the weak and the abuse of power. But a serious critique of capitalism would not be found in Salinger's text even if a full field investigation were ordered. Certainly Holden's fantasy of secluding himself in a cabin in the woods is scarcely a prescription for social activism: "I'd pretend I was one of those deaf-mutes. That way I wouldn't have to have any goddam stupid useless conversations with anybody. If anybody wanted to tell me something, they'd have to write it on a piece of paper and shove it over to me. They'd get bored as hell doing that after a while, and then I'd be through with having conversations for the rest of my life." Such passages will hardly alarm those wishing to repudiate or erase the 1960s, which is why *The Catcher in the Rye* does not belong to the history of dissidence.

Growing Up Absurd (1960) sports a title and a perspective that Holden might have appreciated, but Paul Goodman does not mention the novel. Published at the end of the tumultuous, unpredictable decade, Theodore Roszak's *The Making of a Counter Culture* (which *Newsweek* dubbed "the best guide yet published to the meaning . . . of youthful dissent") likewise fails to mention Salinger, though Holden certainly personifies (or anticipates) "the ethos of disaffiliation that is fiercely obnoxious to the adult society." In 1962 the editor of a collection of critical essays on Salinger—the future editor-in-chief of *Time*—found American campuses innocent of activism: "'Student riots' are a familiar and significant factor in European politics. The phenomenon has no equivalent in the United States." That generalization would soon be falsified. But it should be noted that authors who have fathomed how the 1950s became the 1960s (like Morris Dickstein, Fred Inglis, Maurice Isserman, James Miller) ignore the impact of Salinger's novel.

Because any reading of the novel as a prefiguration of the 1960s is ultimately so unpersuasive, an over-reaction has set in. Alan Nadel, for example, has fashioned Holden into a Cold Warrior, junior division. "Donning his red hunting hat, he attempts to become the good Red-hunter, ferreting out the phonies and the subversives, but in so doing he emulates the bad Red-hunters," Nadel has written. "Uncovering duplicity was the theme of the day," he adds, so that "in thinking constantly about who or what was phony, Caulfield was doing no more than following the instructions of J. Edgar Hoover, the California Board of Regents, *The Nation* [*sic*], the Smith Act, and the Hollywood Ten. . . . Each citizen was potentially both the threat and the threatened." After all, hadn't Gary Cooper, testifying before HUAC, defined Communism as something that was not "on the level"? Nadel equates Caulfield's "disdain for Hollywood" with HUAC's, nor could the young prostitute's mention of Melvyn Douglas have been accidental—since Congressman Richard Nixon had run against Helen Gahagan Douglas, and her husband was himself "a prominent Hollywood liberal." Nadel concludes that "the solution to Caulfield's dilemma becomes renouncing speech itself." Having named names, he realizes: "I sort of *miss* everybody I told about. . . . It's funny. Don't ever tell anybody anything," he advises; that is, don't be an informer. "If you do, you start missing everybody." The narrator "spoke for the cold war HUAC witness," Nadel argued, "expressing existential angst over the nature and meaning of his 'testimony.'" Such an interpretation is far-fetched: Holden is no more interested in politics than his creator, and he's considerably less interested in sanctioning conformity than were the Red-hunters.

Citizens who abhor the 1960s commonly deplore one of its most prominent legacies: the fragmentation into "identity politics," the loss of civic cohesion. Those worrying over this sin also will not find it in Salinger's book, which promotes no class consciousness, racial consciousness, or ethnic consciousness of any sort. Sol Salinger had strayed so far from Judaism that he became an importer of hams and cheeses; and his son left no recognizably Jewish imprint on his fiction. Nor does his novel evoke the special plight of young women and girls. That omission would be rectified about two generations later, when Eve Horowitz's first novel appeared. Her young narrator and protagonist is not only female but emphatically Jewish, and she longs to meet her own Holden Caulfield. Jane Singer recalls: "I hadn't known any males who were as depressed as I was in high school, except for maybe Holden Caulfield, and I didn't really know him." As she's packing to leave Cleveland for Oberlin College, she muses, "besides clothes and shampoo and *The Catcher in the Rye*, I couldn't think of anything else to bring." In her account of growing up female, Horowitz may have wanted to correct the imbalance David Riesman identified in 1961, when, attempting to explain the United States to a Japanese audience, he had commented on the inscrutable popularity of Salinger's novel: "Boys are frustrated because they aren't cowboys, and girls are frustrated because they aren't boys." The sociologist noted that "women have been the audience for American fiction and for movies. There are no girls' stories comparable to *Catcher in the Rye*. Yet girls can adapt themselves and identify with such a book, while a boy can't so easily identify with a girl." In the literary marketplace, Riesman speculated, readers aren't turned off or away if the central characters are male but only if they are female. How many Boy Scouts and Explorer Scouts have been moved by reading *The Bell Jar?*

THE CURSE OF CULTURE

Another way to understand the power of Salinger's novel to generate controversy is to recognize its vulnerability to moralistic criticism. From wherever the source—call it Puritanism, or puritanism, or Victorianism—there persists a tradition of imposing religious standards upon art or of rejecting works of the imagination because they violate conventional ethical codes. According to this legacy, books are neither good nor bad without "for you" being added as a criterion of judgment. This entwining of the aesthetic and the moralistic was obvious as prize committees struggled with the terms of Joseph Pulitzer's instructions that the novels to be honored in his name "shall best present the whole atmosphere of American life." But until 1927, the novels selected more accurately conveyed "the wholesome atmosphere of American life." That eliminated Dreiser. Had the subtle revision of Pulitzer's own intentions not been overturned, virtually all great writers would have been categorically excluded. Nabokov comes quickly to mind. His most famous novel was given to the good family man Adolf Eichmann, then imprisoned in Israel, but was returned after two days with an indignant rejection: *"Das ist aber ein sehr unerfreuliches, Buch"*—quite an unwholesome book. *Lolita* is narrated from the viewpoint of an adult, a pervert whose ornate vocabulary made the novel unintelligible to young readers, and so censors passed it by to target *The Catcher in the Rye*. It is a measure of Salinger's stature among other writers that, though famously dismissive of many literary giants, Nabokov wrote privately of his fellow *New Yorker* contributor: "I do admire him very much."

But the reviewer for *The Christian Science Monitor* did not: *The Catcher in the Rye* "is not fit for children to read"; its central character is "preposterous, profane, and pathetic beyond belief." Too many young readers might even want to emulate Holden, "as too easily happens when immorality and perversion are recounted by writers of talent whose work is countenanced in the name of art or good intention." Here was an early sign of trouble. Nor was respectability enhanced by the novel's first appearance in paperback, for it was offered as pulp fiction, a genre that beckoned with promises of illicit pleasure. The common 1950s practice of issuing serious books in pulp meant that "dozens of classic novels appeared in packages that were cartoonish, sordid or merely absurd." The aim of such marketing, Julie Lasky has suggested, was to grab "the attention of impulse shoppers in drugstores and bus depots; slogans jammed across the four-inch width of paperbound covers compressed the nuances of prizewinning authors into exaggerated come-ons." The 1953 paperback edition of Salinger's novel, for example, assured buyers that "this unusual book may shock you . . . but you will never forget it." The illustration on the cover depicted a prostitute standing near Holden and may have served as the only means by which some citizens judged the book. The cover so offended the author that it contributed to his move to Bantam when his contract with Signet expired. By then, the pulping of classics had largely ended in the wake of hearings by the House of Representatives' Select Committee on Current Pornographic Materials. But the availability of such cheap editions of books ranging from the serious to the lurid drew the curiosity of censors as well as bargain-hunters. The vulnerability of Salinger's novel testified to the aptness of Walter Lippmann's generalization that censorship "is actually applied in proportion to the vividness, the directness, and the intelligibility of the medium which circulates the subversive idea." Movie screens, he wrote in 1927, therefore tend to be more censored than the stage, which is more censored than newspapers and magazines. But "the novel is even freer than the press today because it is an even denser medium of expression." At least that was the case until the paperback revolution facilitated the expansion of the syllabus.

Of course, the paperback revolution was not the only cultural shift affecting the reception of the novel. The career of *The Catcher in the Rye* is virtually synchronous with the Cold War, and Holden Caulfield takes a stand of sorts: he calls himself "a pacifist." For men slightly older than Holden in 1949–50, military conscription was more or less universal, yet he predicts that "it'd drive me crazy if I had to be in the Army. . . . I swear if there's ever another war, they better just take me out and stick me in front of a firing squad. I wouldn't object." Indeed he goes further: "I'm sort of glad they've got the atomic bomb invented. If there's ever another war, I'm going to sit right the hell on top of it. I'll volunteer for it, I swear to God I will." Barely a decade later, Stanley Kubrick's pitch-black comedy *Dr. Strangelove* (1964) would confront nuclear terror by showing Major "King" Kong (Slim Pickens) doing precisely what Holden vows he will step forward to do. With such images in mind, one interpreter has thus boldly claimed that "the fear of nuclear holocaust, not the fear of four-letter words[,]" sparked controversy about *The Catcher in the Rye*.

Salinger's novel may thus also be about history veering out of control, about the abyss into which parents could no longer prevent their offspring from staring, about the impotence to which a can-do people was unaccustomed. "The lack of faith in the American character expressed in the *Catcher* controversies," Professor Pamela Steinle has argued, "is rooted not in doubts about the strength of adolescent Americans' character but in recognition of the powerlessness of American adults—as parents, professionals and community leaders—to provide a genuine sense of the future for the adolescents in their charge." According to Steinle, the novel indicts "adult apathy and complicity in the construction of a social reality in which the American character cannot develop in any meaningful sense beyond adolescence." Nor does the novel warrant any hope that the condition can be remedied. The story is, after all, told from a sanitarium in California—a grim terminus given the common belief that the West offers a second chance. No wonder, then, that John Seelye, who ended his own revised version of *The Adventures of Huckleberry Finn* with Huck's bleakest pessimism ("I didn't much care if the goddam sun never come up again"), could read Salinger's book "as a lengthy suicide note with a blank space at the end to sign your name."

The advantage of Steinle's argument is that she situates the controversy over *The Catcher in the Rye* where it actually took place, which is less in the pages of *Ramparts* than at school board meetings. In such settings, the novel was branded by parents as a threat to their control and heralded by teachers as a measure of their professional autonomy and authority. But the disadvantage of Steinle's view is the scarcity of direct evidence that nuclear fears fueled the debate. Neither those who condemned *The Catcher in the Rye* nor its defenders made the specter of atomic catastrophe pivotal. Neither the moral nor the literary disputes were ventilated in such terms. Compared to

Holden's far more pronounced resistance to maturation, compared to more immediate targets of his scorn, the Bomb hardly registered as a concern among objections to the novel.

But if "the essence of censorship," according to Lippmann, is "not to suppress subversive ideas as such, but to withhold them from those who are young or underprivileged or otherwise undependable," then Steinle's emphasis upon parental assertion of authority is not misplaced. In a more class-conscious society, the Old Bailey prosecutor of the publisher of *Lady Chatterley's Lover* could ask in his opening address to the jury, in 1960: "Is it a book that you would even wish your wife or your servants to read?" But in the United States, overt conflicts are more likely to take generational form; and the first of Lippmann's categories deserves to be highlighted. Some of the books that have arouse the greatest ire place children at the center, like Richard Wright's *Black Boy*, Anne Frank's *Diary of a Young Girl*, and of course *The Adventures of Huckleberry Finn*; and despite the aura of "cuteness" hovering over Salinger's work, it emitted danger by striking at the most vulnerable spot in the hearts of parents. Nor could it have escaped the attention of alert readers that Holden's emotional affiliations are horizontal rather than vertical. His father, a corporate lawyer, is absent from the scene; and his mother is present only as a voice speaking from a dark room. The only relative whom the reader meets is Phoebe, the younger sister (and a mini-Holden).

The contributor's note Salinger submitted to *Harper's* in 1946 was his credo: "I almost always write about very young people"; and the directness with which he spoke *to* them had much to do with his appeal—and with the anxiety that his literary intervention provoked in the internecine battle between generations. The effectiveness of his empathy posed a challenge to parents who invoked their right to be custodians of the curriculum, and the "legions of decency" may have sensed "a unique seductive power" which Salinger's biographer claims *The Catcher in the Rye* exudes. Even if the less sensitive or eccentric of its young readers might not try to assume Holden's persona, at least teenagers could imitate his lingo. A book that elicits such proprietary interest—succeeding cohorts believing in a special access to Salinger's meaning—was bound to arouse some suspicion that conventional authority was being outflanked. Salinger's adroit fidelity to the feelings and experiences of his protagonist was what made the novel so tempting a target. Perhaps *The Catcher in the Rye* has been banned precisely because it is so cherished; because it is so easily loved, some citizens love to hate it.

Steinle has closely examined the local controversies that erupted over the book in Alabama, Virginia, New Mexico, and California as well as the debates conducted in such publications as the *PTA Magazine* and the

Newsletter on Intellectual Freedom of the American Library Association. She discovered a "division . . . over whether to prepare adolescents for or to protect them from adult disillusionment. . . . In the postwar period . . . recognition of the increasing dissonance between American ideals and the realities of social experience has become unavoidable, and it is precisely this cultural dissonance that is highlighted by Salinger's novel." Its literary value got lost in the assertion of family values, in a campaign that must be classified as reactionary. "They say it describes reality," a parent in Boron, California, announced. "I say let's back up from reality. Let's go backwards. Let's go back to when we didn't have an immoral society." When so idyllic a state existed was not specified, but what is evident is the element of anti-intellectualism that the struggle against permissiveness entailed. Here some of the parents were joined by Leonard Hall, the school superintendent of Bay County, Florida, who warned in 1987 against assigning books that were not state-approved because, he sagely opined, reading "is where you get ideas from."

Attempts at vindication were occasionally made on the same playing field that censors themselves chose. Though Holden labels himself "sort of an atheist," he could be praised as a saint, if admittedly a picaresque one. One educator discerned in the protagonist a diamond in the rough: "He befriends the friendless. He respects those who are humble, loyal, and kind. He demonstrates a strong love for his family" (or for Phoebe anyway). Besides enacting such New Testament teachings, "he abhors hypocrisy. He values sex that comes from caring for another person and rejects its sordidness. And, finally, he wants to be a responsible member of society, to guide and protect those younger than he." But a character witness is not the same as a literary critic, and such conflation seems to have gained little traction when the right of English teachers to make up reading lists was contested. If Holden's defense rested on a sanitized version of his character, then the implication was that assigned books with less morally meritorious protagonists might be subject to parental veto. Such a defense also assumed that disgruntled parents were themselves exegetes who had simply misread a text, that community conflicts could be resolved by more subtle interpretations. There is no reason to believe, however, that the towns where the novel was banned or challenged overlapped with maps of misreading. But such communities *were* places where parents tried to gain control of the curriculum, which is why *The Catcher in the Rye* would still have been proscribed even had it been re-read as a book of virtues.

For the objections that were most frequently raised were directed at the novelist's apparent desire to capture profuse adolescent profanity in the worst way. In the *Catholic World*, reviewer Riley Hughes disliked the narrator's "excessive use of amateur swearing and coarse language," which made his character simply "monotonous." According to one angry parent's tabulation, 237 instances of "goddamn," 58 uses of the synonym for a person of illegitimate birth, 31 "Chrissakes," and one incident of flatulence constituted what was wrong with Salinger's book. Though blasphemy is not a crime, *The Catcher in the Rye* "uses the Lord's name in vain two hundred times," an opponent in Boron asserted—"enough [times] to ban it right there." The statistics are admittedly not consistent. But it is incontestable that the text contains six examples of "fuck" or "fuck you," though here Holden is actually allied with the censorious parents, since he does not swear with this four-letter word himself but instead tries to efface it from walls. He's indignant that children should be subjected to such graffiti. Upon seeing the word even in the Egyptian tomb room at the Metropolitan Museum of Art, however, Holden achieves a melancholy and mature insight that such offenses to dignity cannot really be expunged from the world: "You can't ever find a place that's nice and peaceful, because there isn't any."

What happened to *The Catcher in the Rye* wasn't always nice and peaceful because it took a linguistic turn. Though historians are fond of defining virtually every era as one of transition, it does make sense to locate the publication of Salinger's novel on the cusp of change. The novel benefited from the loosening of tongues that the Second World War sanctioned, yet the profanity in which Holden indulges still looked conspicuous before the 1960s. Salinger thus helped to accelerate the trend toward greater freedom for writers but found himself the target of those offended by the adolescent vernacular still rarely enough recorded in print. During the Second World War, the Production Code had been slightly relaxed for *We Are the Marines*. This 1943 *March of Time* documentary was permitted to use mild expletives like "damn" "under stress of battle conditions." Professor Thomas Doherty adds that, "in the most ridiculed example of the Code's tender ears, Noel Coward's *In Which We Serve* (1942), a British import, was held up from American release for seventeen words: ten 'damns,' two 'hells,' two 'Gods,' two 'bastards,' and one 'lousy.'"

Only three years before publication of Salinger's novel, homophonic language was inserted into Norman Mailer's *The Naked and the Dead* at the suggestion of his cousin, Charles Rembar. A crackerjack First Amendment attorney who would later represent such clients as Fanny Hill and Constance Chatterley, Rembar proposed the substitution of *fug* (as in "Fug you. Fug the goddam gun") partly because the president of the house publishing the novel feared his own mother's reaction. The U.S. Information Agency was nevertheless unpersuaded and banned Mailer's book from its overseas libraries. As late as 1952, the revised edition of *Webster's Unabridged* offered a simple but opaque definition of masturbation as "onanism; self-pollution."

The next year President Eisenhower delivered a celebrated plea at Dartmouth College: "Don't join the book-burners. . . . Don't be afraid to go into your library and read every book." His amendment is less cited—"as long as that document does not offend our own ideas of decency." Though the war in which Mailer and Salinger fought allowed some indecorous terms to go public, the 1960 Presidential debates included the spectacle of Nixon seeking to trump another ex-sailor by promising the electorate—after Harry Truman's salty lapses—to continue Ike's restoration of "decency and, frankly, good language" in the White House.

In this particular war of words, Salinger was conscripted into a cause for which he was no more suited than any other. If he was affiliated with any institution at all, it was the *New Yorker*, which initially published his *Nine Stories* as well as the substance of his two subsequent books. In that magazine even the mildest profanity was strictly forbidden, and editorial prudishness would have spiked publication of excerpts from the final version of what became his most admired work. It may be plausible, as one scholar circling the text has noted, that "the radical nature of Salinger's portrayal of disappointment with American society, so much like Twain's in *Huck Finn*, was probably as much of the reason that *Catcher* (like *Huck*) was banned from schools and colleges as were the few curse words around which the battle was publicly fought." But such ideological objections to Salinger's novel were rarely raised, much less articulated with any cogency; and therefore no historian of the reception of this book should minimize the salience of those "few curse words."

Could *The Catcher in the Rye* have avoided the turbulent pool into which it was so often sucked? Could the novel have been rescued from primitive detractors and retained an even more secure status in the public school curriculum? One compromise was never considered. It is the solution that Noah Webster commonly applied to dictionaries and spelling books, that Emerson recommended to Whitman for *Leaves of Grass*, and that Lewis Carroll intended to enact with a volume entitled *The Girl's Own Shakespeare*: expurgation. Had Holden's lingo been sanitized in accordance with the legacy of Dr. Thomas Bowdler, the moral (or moralistic) resistance to Salinger's novel would have evaporated. Bowdlerization constitutes what its leading student has called "literary slum clearance," but it also cordons off the censors. Of course Holden would not have been Holden with expletives deleted. The guileless integrity of his language makes him so memorable and therefore the novel so distinctive. Richard Watson Gilder had inflicted the kindest cuts of all on Huck's talk, but by the 1950s no expurgators survived to spare Holden from the animosity he incurred. Such an explanation may be too obvious and all, if you really want to know. It's so simple it kills me, for Chrissake. But I really believe it's the best explanation. I really do.

Chronology

1919   Jerome David Salinger is born in New York City on January 1, to Sol Salinger, a prosperous Jewish meat and cheese importer, and Miriam Jillich Salinger, a woman of Scottish-Irish descent.

1934   Enrolls in Valley Forge Military Academy, in Pennsylvania.

1936   Graduates from Valley Forge Military Academy.

1938   Travels in Europe and begins writing short stories.

1939   Takes a short story writing course taught by Whit Burnett at Columbia University.

1940   First short story, "The Young Folks," published in *Story*, the magazine Whit Burnett edits.

1941   Sells first story about Holden Caulfield to the *New Yorker* but publication is delayed until after World War II.

1942   Drafted into United States Army and attends Officers, First Sergeants, and Instructors School of the Signal Corps.

1943   Stationed in Nashville, Tennessee, achieving the rank of staff sergeant. Transferred to the Army Counter-Intelligence Corps. Short story "The Varioni Brothers" published in the *Saturday Evening Post*.

1944   Transferred to Europe with the U.S. Army Fourth Infantry Division. Lands at Utah Beach, Normandy with D-Day invasion forces and participates in the liberation of France. Serves as Security Agent for the Twelfth Infantry Regiment.

1945　　　Discharged from the Army.

1945–47　　Publishes stories in the *Saturday Evening Post, Colliers, Esquire,*
　　　　　　and the *New Yorker.* Writes a story about Holden Caulfield,
　　　　　　"Slight Rebellion Off Madison," that is later incorporated into
　　　　　　The Catcher in the Rye. Writes a ninety-page novella about
　　　　　　Holden Caulfield that he withdraws from consideration for
　　　　　　publication.

1948–50　　Publishes his major short stories in the *New Yorker,* including "A
　　　　　　Perfect Day for Bananafish," "Uncle Wiggily in Connecticut,"
　　　　　　"Just before the War with the Eskimos," "The Laughing Man,"
　　　　　　and "For Esmé—with Love and Squalor."

1950　　　Film version of "Uncle Wiggily in Connecticut," *My Foolish
　　　　　　Heart* starring Susan Hayward and Dana Andrews, released by
　　　　　　Samuel Goldwyn Studio. Salinger studies Indian thought at
　　　　　　Sumitra Paniter Ramakrishna Vivekananda Center in New York
　　　　　　City.

1951　　　*The Catcher in the Rye* published in July. "Pretty Mouth and
　　　　　　Green My Eyes" appears in the *New Yorker.*

1953　　　Moves to a country house in the remote village of Cornish,
　　　　　　New Hampshire. Publishes "Teddy" in the *New Yorker. Nine
　　　　　　Stories* appears in April. Meets Claire Douglas.

1955　　　Marries Claire Douglas on February 17. "Raise High the Roof
　　　　　　Beam, Carpenters" and "Franny" are published in the *New
　　　　　　Yorker.* A daughter, Margaret Ann, is born on December 10.

1957–59　　"Zooey" and "Seymour: An Introduction" published in the *New
　　　　　　Yorker.*

1960　　　A son, Matthew, born on February 13.

1961　　　*Franny and Zooey* published.

1963　　　*Raise High the Roof Beam, Carpenters* and *Seymour: An
　　　　　　Introduction* published.

1965　　　Publishes "Hapworth 16, 1924" in the *New Yorker.*

1967　　　Divorced. Lives in seclusion and refuses contact with public life.

1974　　　Salinger takes legal action to suppress the unauthorized
　　　　　　Complete Uncollected Short Stories of J. D. Salinger in his only
　　　　　　public statement in years.

1987   Salinger brings a lawsuit against Ian Hamilton for unauthorized
        use of his unpublished correspondence in *J. D. Salinger: A
        Writing Life*. He wins the suit and the biography is published
        the following year in severely truncated form.

Contributors

HAROLD BLOOM is Sterling Professor of the Humanities at Yale University and Henry W. and Albert A. Berg Professor of English at the New York University Graduate School. He is the author of over 20 books, including *The Anxiety of Influence* (1973), which sets forth Professor Bloom's provocative theory of the literary relationships between the great writers and their predecessors. His most recent book, *Shakespeare: The Invention of the Human* (1998), was a finalist for the 1998 National Book Award. Professor Bloom is a 1985 MacArthur Foundation Award recipient, served as the Charles Eliot Norton Professor of Poetry at Harvard University in 1987–88, and has received honorary degrees from the universities of Rome and Bologna. In 1999, Professor Bloom received the prestigious American Academy of Arts and Letters Gold Medal for Criticism.

ARTHUR HEISERMAN (1929–1975) was Professor of English at the University of Chicago. He is the author of *Skelton and Satire* (1961) and *The Novel before the Novel: Essays and Discussions about the Beginnings of Prose Fiction in the West* (1977).

JAMES E. MILLER JR. is former Professor of English at the University of Chicago. He is the author of many books of criticism, including *Start with the Sun: Studies in Cosmic Poetry* (1960), *Quests Surd and Absurd* (1967), and *The American Quest for a Supreme Fiction* (1979). He has also published critical studies of Herman Melville, Walt Whitman, T. S. Eliot, F. Scott Fitzgerald, and J. D. Salinger, and edited numerous volumes.

DONALD COSTELLO is former Professor of American Studies at the University of Notre Dame. He is the author of *The Serpent's Eye: Shaw and the Cinema* (1965) and *Fellini's Road* (1983).

CLINTON W. TROWBRIDGE is former Professor of English at Adelphi Suffolk College. He has published essays on Flannery O'Connor, Saul Bellow, and Arthur Miller.

JAMES BRYAN has published several essays on Salinger's short fiction, as well as essays on William Dean Howells, Ernest Hemingway, and Sherwood Anderson.

KERRY McSWEENEY is Professor of English at McGill University. She is the author of *The Language of the Senses* (1998) and *Supreme Attachments: Studies in Victorian Love Poetry* (1998), and has also published critical studies of George Eliot, Herman Melville, and Ralph Ellison.

EDWIN HAVILAND MILLER is former Professor of English at New York University. He is the author of *Walt Whitman's Poetry: A Psychological Journey* (1968), *Melville* (1975), and *Walt Whitman's "Song of Myself": A Mosaic of Interpretations* (1989).

ALAN NADEL is the author of *Containment Culture: American Narratives, Postmodernism, and the Atomic Age* (1995), *Flatlining on the Field of Dreams: Cultural Narratives in the Films of President Reagan's America* (1997), and *Invisible Criticism: Ralph Ellison and the American Canon* (1988). In 1993, he won the William Riley Parker prize for the best essay in *PMLA*.

A. ROBERT LEE is the editor of many volumes of criticism of American and Afro-American literature, and has most recently published *Designs of Blackness* (1998).

JOYCE ROWE is Assistant Professor of English at Fordham University. She is the author of *Equivocal Endings in Classic American Novels* (1988).

DENNIS McCORT is Associate Professor of Languages, Literatures, and Linguistics at Syracuse University. He is the author of several articles on German romanticism and on the relation of zen to literature.

STEPHEN J. WHITFIELD holds the Max Richter Chair in American Civilization at Brandeis University. He is the author of *American Space, Jewish Time* (1988) and *The Culture of the Cold War* (1991).

Bibliography

Baumbach, Jonathan. "The Saint as a Young Man: A Reappraisal of *The Catcher in the Rye*." *Modern Language Quarterly* 25 (1964): 461–72.

Belcher, William F., and James W. Lee, eds. *J. D. Salinger and the Critics*. Belmont, CA: Wadsworth, 1962.

Bloom, Harold, ed. *Holden Caulfield*. New York: Chelsea House, 1990.

———. *J. D. Salinger*. New York: Chelsea House, 1987.

Burrows, David J. "Allie and Phoebe: Death and Love in Salinger's *The Catcher in the Rye*." In *Private Dealings: Modern American Writers in Search of Integrity*. Eds. David J. Burrows, Lewis M. Dabney, Milne Holton, and Grosvenor E. Powell. Rockville, MD: Almquist and Wiksell, 1969, pp. 106–14.

Carpenter, F. I. "The Adolescent in American Fiction." *English Journal* 46 (1957): 313–19.

Cohen, Hubert I. "'A Woeful Agony Which Forceed Me to Begin My Tale': *The Catcher in the Rye*." *Modern Fiction Studies* 12 (Fall 1966): 355–66.

Edwards, Duane. "Holden Caulfield: 'Don't Ever Tell Anybody Anything.'" *English Literary History* 44 (1977): 556–67.

French, Warren. *J. D. Salinger*. New York: Twayne, 1963.

———. *J. D. Salinger, Revisited*. Boston: Hall, 1988.

Furst, Lilian R. "Dostoyevsky's *Notes from the Underground* and Salinger's *The Catcher in the Rye*." *Canadian Review of Comparative Literature* 5 (1978): 72–85.

Glasser, William. "*The Catcher in the Rye*." *Michigan Quarterly Review* 15 (1976): 432–57.

Goodman, Anne. Review of *The Catcher in the Rye*, "Mad about Children." *New Republic* 125 (16 July 1951): 20–21.

Grunwald, Henry Anatole, ed. *Salinger: A Critical and Personal Portrait*. New York: Harper and Brothers, 1962.

Hamilton, Ian. *A Search for J. D. Salinger*. New York: Random House, 1988.

Hamilton, Kenneth. *J. D. Salinger: A Critical Essay*. Grand Rapids, MI: Eerdmans, 1967.

Hassan, Ihab. "The Victim: Images of Evil in Recent American Fiction." *College English* 21 (1959–60): 140–46.

Howell, John M. "Salinger in the Waste Land." *Modern Fiction Studies* 12 (Autumn 1966): 367–75.

Jones, Ernest. Review of *The Catcher in the Rye*, "Case History of All of Us." *Nation* 173, no. 9 (1 September 1951): 176.

Laser, Marvin, and Norman Fruman, ed. *Studies of J. D. Salinger: Reviews, Essays, and Critiques of* The Catcher in the Rye *and Other Fiction*. New York: Odyssey Press, 1963.

Longstreth, T. Morris. Review of *The Catcher in the Rye*. *Christian Science Monitor* (19 July 1951).

Luedtke, Luther S. "J. D. Salinger and Robert Burns: The Catcher in the Rye." *Modern Fiction Studies* 16 (1970): 198–201.

Lundquist, James. *J. D. Salinger*. New York: Ungar, 1979.

Marsden, Malcolm M., ed. *If You Really Want to Know: A* Catcher *Casebook*. Chicago: Scott, Foresman, 1963.

Medovoi, Leerom. "Democracy, Capitalism, and American Literature: The Cold War Construction of J. D. Salinger's Paperback Hero." *The Other Fifties: Interrogating Midcentury American Icons*. Ed. Joel Foreman. Urbana, IL: University of Illinois Press, 1997.

Mellard, James M. "The Disappearing Subject: A Lacanian Reading of *The Catcher in the Rye*." In *Critical Essays on Salinger's* The Catcher in the Rye. Ed. Joel Salzberg. Boston: Hall, 1990.

Meral, Jean. "The Ambiguous Mr. Antolini in Salinger's *Catcher in the Rye*." *Caliban* 7 (1970): 55–58.

Miller, James E. Jr. "*Catcher* in and out of History." *Critical Inquiry* 3, no. 3 (Spring 1977): 599–603.

Modern Fiction Studies 12.3 (Autumn 1966). Special Salinger number.

Ohmann, Carol, and Richard Ohmann. "Reviewers, Critics and *The Catcher in the Rye*." *Critical Inquiry* 3, no. 1 (Autumn 1976): 15–37.

———. "Universals and the Historically Particular." *Critical Inquiry* 3, no. 4 (Summer 1977): 773–77.

Oldsey, Bernard S. "The Movies in the Rye." *College English* 23 (1961): 209–15.

Peavy, Charles D. "'Did You Ever Have a Sister?': Holden, Quentin, and Sexual Innocence." *Florida Quarterly* 1 (1968): 82–95.

Pinsker, Sanford. The Catcher in the Rye: *Innocence under Pressure*. New York: Twayne, 1993.

Rosen, Gerald. "A Retrospective Look at *The Catcher in the Rye*." *American Quarterly* 29 (1977): 547–62.

———. *Zen in the Art of J. D. Salinger*. Berkeley: Creative Art Books Co., 1977.

Salzberg, Joel, ed. *Critical Essays on Salinger's* The Catcher in the Rye. Boston: Hall, 1990.

Salzman, Jack, ed. *New Essays on* The Catcher in the Rye. New York: Cambridge University Press, 1991.

Schriber, Mary Suzanne. "Holden Caulfield, C'est Moi." In *Critical Essays on Salinger's* The Catcher in the Rye. Ed. Joel Salzberg. Boston: Hall, 1990.

Simonson, Harold P., and Phillip E. Hager, ed. *Salinger's* Catcher in the Rye: *Clamor vs. Criticism*. Lexington, MA: D. C. Heath, 1963.

Smith, Harrison. Review of *The Catcher in the Rye*, "Manhattan Ulysses, Junior." *Saturday Review* 34, no. 28 (14 July 1951): 12–13.

Stashower, Daniel M. "On First Looking into Chapman's Holden: Speculations on a Murder." *American Scholar* 52 (1982–83): 373–77.

Strauch, Carl F. "Kings in the Back Row: Meaning through Structure—A Reading of Salinger's *The Catcher in the Rye*." *Wisconsin Studies in Contemporary Literature* 2 (Winter 1961): 5–30.

Sublette, Jack R. *J. D. Salinger: An Annotated Bibliography 1938–1981*. New York: Garland, 1984.

Vail, Dennis. "Holden and Psychoanalysis." *PMLA* 91 (1976): 120–21.

Vanderbilt, Kermit. "Symbolic Resolution in *The Catcher in the Rye:* The Cap, the Carrousel, and the American West." *Western Humanities Review* 17 (1963): 271–77.

Wells, Arvin R. "Huck Finn and Holden Caulfield: The Situation of the Hero." *Ohio University Review* 1 (1960): 31–42.

Wenke, John. *J. D. Salinger: A Study of the Short Fiction*. Boston: Twayne, 1991.

Wiegand, William. "The Knighthood of J. D. Salinger." *The New Republic* 141 (19 October 1959): 19–21.

Wisconsin Studies in Contemporary Literature 4.1 (Winter 1963). Special Salinger number.

Zapf, Hubert. "Logical Action in *The Catcher in the Rye*." *College Literature* 12 (1985): 266–71.

Acknowledgements

"J. D. Salinger: Some Crazy Cliff" by Arthur Heiserman and James E. Miller Jr. From *Western Humanities Review* 10:2 (Spring 1956): 129–37. © 1956 University of Utah. Reprinted by permission.

"The Language of *The Catcher in the Rye*" by Donald P. Costello. From *American Speech* 34:3 (October 1959): 172–81. © 1959. All rights reserved. Reprinted by permission of Duke University Press.

"The Symbolic Structure of *The Catcher in the Rye*" by Clinton W. Trowbridge. First published in the *Sewanee Review*, Vol. 74, no. 3 (Summer 1966): 681–93. © 1966 The University of the South. Reprinted with the permission of the editor.

"The Psychological Structure of *The Catcher in the Rye*" by James Bryan. From *PMLA* 89:5 (October 1974): 1065–74. © 1974 The Modern Language Association of America. Reprinted by permission of the Modern Language Association of America.

"Salinger Revisited" by Kerry McSweeney. From *Critical Quarterly* 20:1 (Spring 1978): 61–68. © 1978 Manchester University Press. Reprinted by permission.

"In Memoriam: Allie Caulfield in *The Catcher in the Rye*" by Edwin Haviland Miller. From *Mosaic* 15:1 (Winter 1982): 129–40. © 1982 *Mosaic*. Reprinted by permission.

"Rhetoric, Sanity, and the Cold War: The Significance of Holden Caulfield's Testimony" by Alan Nadel. From *Centennial Review* 32:4 (Fall 1988): 351–71. © 1988 *The Centennial Review*. Reprinted by permission.

"'Flunking Everything Else Except English Anyway': Holden Caulfield, Author" by A. Robert Lee. From *Critical Essays on Salinger's* The Catcher in the Rye, ed. Joel Salzberg. © 1990 Joel Salzberg. Reprinted by permission of Cambridge University Press.

"Holden Caulfield and American Protest" by Joyce Rowe. From *New Essays on* The Catcher in the Rye, ed. Jack Salzman. © 1991 Cambridge University Press. Reprinted by permission of Cambridge University Press.

Dennis McCort, "Hyakujo's Geese, Amban's Doughnuts, and Rilke's Carrousel: Sources East and West for Salinger's Catcher," *Comparative Literature Studies* 34:3 (1997): 260–78. © 1997 by the Pennsylvania State University. Reprinted by permission of the publishers.

The New England Quarterly, v. 70 (December 1997; 567–600) for"Cherished and Cursed Toward a Social History of *The Catcher in the Rye* by Stephen J. Whitfield. © 1997 by the New England Quarterly. Reproduced by permission of the publisher and author.

Index